BEYONCÉ

IN

FORMATION

Beyoncé in Formation

Remixing Black Feminism

Omise'eke Natasha Tinsley

UNIVERSITY OF TEXAS PRESS ꙮ AUSTIN

Requests for permission to reproduce material
from this work should be sent to:
Permissions
University of Texas Press
P.O. Box 7819
Austin, TX 78713-7819
utpress.utexas.edu/rp-form

♾ The paper used in this book meets the minimum requirements
of ANSI/NISO Z39.48-1992 (R1997) (Permanence of Paper).

Names: Tinsley, Omise'eke Natasha, 1971- author.
Title: Beyoncé in formation : remixing black feminism /
Omise'eke Natasha Tinsley.
Description: Austin : University of Texas, 2018.
Includes bibliographical references and index.
Identifiers: LCCN 2018014320
ISBN 978-1-4773-1839-3 (pbk. : alk. paper)
ISBN 978-1-4773-1771-6 (library e-book)
ISBN 978-1-4773-1772-3 (non-library e-book)
Subjects: LCSH: Beyoncé, 1981- | African American women singers.
African American feminists. | Feminism and music.
Classification: LCC ML420.K675 T56 2018 |
DDC 782.42164092--dc23
LC record available at https://lccn.loc.gov/2018014320

doi:10.7560/318393

For my Queen Bee,
Baía

CONTENTS

BEYONCÉ
IN
FORMATION

INTRODUCTION
FOR THE TEXAS BAMA FEMME

On April 4, 2008, while spring pushed into full blossom, Beyoncé Knowles and Jay Z Carter wed in a private ceremony at the groom's light-bathed, 8,309-square-foot Tribeca penthouse. One hundred thousand white orchids were flown in from Thailand, forty guests driven to the penthouse by private chauffeurs, and a large rooftop tent decked in royal-themed decorations for the occasion. Beyoncé's mother Tina and Jay Z's grandmother Hattie home-cooked a Southern feast, and Tina designed the bride's strapless, floor-length white gown. As Knowles family pastor Rudy Rasmus led the couple in their vows, Jay Z slipped a $5 million, 18-carat Lorraine Schwartz diamond ring on the bride's finger. The newlyweds waited six months to speak to the press about their wedding but when they did, Beyoncé described married life in superlatives as brilliantly glowing as her ring. "People feel like they lose something when they get married, but it doesn't have to be that way. There's nothing more exciting than having a witness to your life," she said, smiling. "When you find the person that you trust and you love and you feel is going to respect you and take all the shit that you have and turn it around and bring out the best in you, it feeds you. It is the most powerful thing you can ever feel in your life."[1]

My life isn't very much like Beyoncé's; my wedding wasn't, either. On the icy morning of November 20, 2011, Matt Richardson and I were joined in legal matrimony at Hennepin County Court in Minneapolis, Minnesota. I walked down the aisle in a blue sweater dress and stiletto heels that, together, cost as much as five orchids at Beyoncé's wedding. Our two-year-old daughter Baía, in Afro-puffs and a pink ruffled sweater dress, served as ring bearer; my ring was a $275

1

vintage gold band with a blue topaz—Matt's birthstone—surrounded by two small aquamarines—my birthstone. Despite a driver's license identifying him as "male" Matt, who legally transitioned the year Baía was born, was nervous about passing for the judge (who offered her unsolicited opinions on lesbian weddings). But we were pronounced husband and wife without incident and, after receiving the judge's words of advice for happy married life, celebrated with a small lunch hosted by a friend. When Matt and I met as graduate students at UC Berkeley, not only did neither of us imagine we'd marry each other; as radical black lesbian feminists with a strong critique of legal marriage—an institution we were barred from at the time—neither of us imagined we'd marry anyone. Matt coauthored an article titled "Is Gay Marriage Racist?," whose deconstruction of marriage sounds nothing like Beyoncé's rose-colored description: "Not every queer desires to base their family on the model of the two-parent household with 2.5 kids. Every time white lesbian and gay leaders trot out some well-heeled homosexual couple who own their own homes, have six figure salaries, and live the American dream, they do violence to the numerous forms of intimate partnerships and loving parenting that do not conform to mainstream ideas."[2] Go ahead, baby, tell the truth and shame the devil.

So why did Matt and I marry? We both still believe idealizing matrimony does violence to the many creative ways black people love each other and make families. And we're under no illusion our ability to marry proves there's hope or acceptance for black queers like us. Honestly, if Baía hadn't graced my life, I don't think I would've felt the need to marry. But praise my guardian angels, she did. And praise my guardian angels, in fall 2011—when I was offered a professorship in the Department of African and African Diaspora Studies at the University of Texas at Austin, where Matt had lived and worked since 2006—I was the mother of a two-year-old girl

I was about to move from her native blue state, across the Mason-Dixon line my grandparents so eagerly left in the dust, to blood-red Texas. I didn't know what living in the South would be like, really, but maybe a marriage license would help Baía grow up with another inch of safety around her. Maybe a marriage license beside her birth certificate would send teachers and doctors and child welfare workers a message that this is a child who's loved, who's cared for, whose life matters. A few nights after my job interview, my great-grandmother Arties came to me in a dream. Before I crossed state lines to follow anyone, she told me without mincing words, I needed to marry them. She moved from Goodwater, Alabama, to Birmingham to marry, just to make sure she'd never end up a farmer's wife; and (she pointed out) I wasn't too smart or too cute to need the security marriage could bring a black woman, either. If I wanted to join Matt in Texas, well, I needed to put a ring on it.

So I arrived in a sunny Texas winter as a madly-in-love, hopeful newlywed who never imagined she'd be anyone's wife and had no idea how to be one. Now, folks around me seemed to have ideas about what my wedding ring meant. People hailed me as "Mrs. Richardson" or called Matt "Mr. Tinsley," repairmen addressed me as the lady of the house before asking to speak to my husband, straight black couples smiled in recognition on the street, and Baía's friends' mothers talked to me about kitchen cleaning, kid-friendly recipes, and bathing suits husbands will go crazy for. One afternoon coming back from Baía's ballet class, we passed a billboard that shouted in large block letters TEXAS MOMS—and this Bay Area–born, radical black queer feminist suddenly realized, *that's me.*

So it's no coincidence that shortly after I moved to Austin, I fell into a deep, longing, starry-eyed fascination with another Texas mom: Houston native Beyoncé Knowles-Carter, whose daughter Blue was born the winter I moved to her home state.

Mrs. Carter (as Beyoncé's tour was named at the time) was the kind of Texas mom I desired, yes, and the kind I desired to be: a black wife-and-mother who never appeared on stage with her legs covered, extolled the virtues of her ass, and sang flanked by black women dancers and her all-female band the Sugar Mamas. While I know Beyoncé Giselle Knowles is a flesh-and-blood human born September 4, 1981, I've never had the pleasure of meeting her. The Beyoncé *I* know is a character created in her songs and videos—an unapologetically regal, overflowingly sensual, divinely hyperfeminine character I adore. In February 2014, Beyoncé released an extended promo video for her "Mrs. Carter" tour that crystallizes this character for me.[3] Laced into a gold corset and gold hoop sans skirt, dripping with chains and jewels, brandishing a scepter and balancing a crown on her curls, Beyoncé emerges from behind double doors and glides into the halls of a Versailles-like palace where she reigns as Sun Queen. No place in the "real" world, this is the jewel-laden, spectacularly abundant fantasy of a black feminist imagination: an alternative (un)reality where black women *are our own wealth*, where our sexuality can glitter as openly as an unskirted gold hoop and the corset designed to rein in our womanness transforms into a display of powerful self-creation. I watched this promo and videos from the self-titled album Beyoncé performed on the tour so often that one day Baía threw out in exasperation: "You just want to marry Beyoncé but you can't, *because she's already married!*" Not because same-sex marriage was illegal in Texas, mind you, or because I'd never met the woman, but because Jay Z got there first. *Well.*

My years as a new wife were also my years as a new professor at UT Austin. Teaching black studies and women's and gender studies there, it quickly became apparent how eager students were for entry-level classes to black feminism. So I put my mind to developing one. After offering a black women writers' course that enrolled only a few students, I dusted myself off and tried again. For spring 2015, I listed a course titled Beyoncé Feminism, Rihanna Womanism. Here students were promised a chance to engage the music of Beyoncé and Rihanna as popular, accessible expressions of black feminisms, texts that offer opportunities to reflect on what black womanness means in our own lives. And students *showed up*, over-enrolling the class until we found a larger lecture hall we also filled to capacity. On the first day of lecture, lines of black women and queers approached me to express excitement that they were in a class that took Beyoncé's music *seriously*. That someone was reflecting back that the lyrics they sing, the songs they dance to, their shirts that proclaim "I woke up like this" just might be important and worthwhile— just might be the meaningful sources of empowerment they always felt them to be. Greeting this receiving line of feminist Beyoncé fans, I saw clearly: I'm just one of thousands of black women and queers in Texas looking to Beyoncé as a gilded mirror, an artistic creation with the capacity to bounce light off our visions for next-millennium feminism.

The first two years of the course were built around Beyoncé's solo albums from *Dangerously in Love* to *Beyoncé*. But on April 23, 2016, *Lemonade* changed everything. Departing from the wide-ranging locations of her self-titled album, this surprise visual album lavishly offered what I'd been searching for in Beyoncé's music in the first place: a vision of unapologetically black, unapologetically feminist lives situated in the historical, artistic, and political landscape of the US South. "Beyoncé is country as cornbread. As bamafied as okra and stewed tomatoes, watermelon with salt, grits, and gravy. She is sweet as honeysuckle nectar, as hot as the chow-chow that goes on your greens," Terryn Hall praises. "Numberless debates after the release of her hotly anticipated visual album *Lemonade*, one thing is strikingly, abundantly clear: Beyoncé is black, and Southern, down to her very core."[4] And for those of us who are queer black women living in the South, *Lemonade* offers another kind of celebration. Its visual landscape is flooded with black Southern women loving each other fiercely, tenderly, and daily on front porches, at kitchen tables, and in plantation bedrooms. Sydney Gore hails *Lemonade* as "A Love Letter From Beyoncé To Black Women" and Hall tellingly compares it to Alice Walker's *The Color Purple*.[5] "The love between Celie and the women in her life is the same thick love that Beyoncé shows to her tribe of women in this film," she writes.[6] Here it was, a gift as abundant and Texan as bluebonnets in March: a text overflowing with visions of what it looks like to be black, married, a mother, and a woman who loves women in the South.

So when Casey Kittrell at University of Texas Press approached me, kindly inquiring if I might have an idea for a book about Beyoncé, I did. *Beyoncé in Formation: Remixing Black Feminism* takes up Beyoncé's invitation to consider the US South as a fertile site for black women to reimagine gender, sexuality, and personhood. At once a popular music study and a memoir, this book puts *Lemonade* in conversation with representations of black Southern femininities from blues to New Orleans bounce, quadroon balls to the Country Music Awards, and *Love and Hip Hop: Atlanta* to #BlackTransLivesMatter. *Beyoncé in Formation* takes up a number of black feminist questions I've asked myself and my students over the last five years. Watching Beyoncé lament the state of marriage, I ask: How do black women celebrate our partnerships while still resisting heterocentric norms that have never served us? Seeing Beyoncé reflect on reproductive violence against black women in the South, I question: How can we embrace "revolutionary mothering" in times and places hostile to our children's survival? Watching Queen Bey give the world her middle finger, I wonder: What does it mean to refuse to act like the "ladies" our Southern grandmothers hoped we'd become—to resist respectability politics even as we demand respect for the unconventional ways we walk through the world? Seeing Beyoncé curate memorable cameos by Southern black women ranging from Sybrina Fulton to Quvenzhané Wallis, I contemplate: How do black women create space to prioritize, embody, and enjoy the love of other black women amid an onslaught of media that attempts to convince us we're unlovable?

Lemonade provides no answers to such questions. But, as (arguably) the most widely distributed black feminist text of the current moment, it offers a spectacular entry point into black feminist artistic, theoretical, and activist conversations that rarely get airtime in dominant imaginations. *Beyoncé in Formation* draws on *Lemonade*'s cornucopia of images of homegrown, hip-switching, cornrowed black femininities, to splice together a mixtape-like vision of black queer Southern feminism from snippets of popular culture, academic texts, and personal experiences. All the musical, academic, and personal sources I draw on have holes, flaws, and inconsistencies, leaving my black feminist mixtape with gaps and missed beats. But refusing to tie up these messy transitions becomes part of the book's black feminist praxis, as I consider how unfinished visions like Beyoncé's offer space for black women to creatively reinvent our genders, pleasures, and alliances in unexpected ways.

BEYONCÉ FEMME-INISM

Maybe you've read this far and you're wondering: Mrs. Richardson—just kidding, I mean Omise'eke—as a feminist and an academic, why are you so celebratory of Beyoncé? Is she even a feminist, really? The debates over whether Beyoncé deserves the title "feminist" have, I admit, exasperated and intrigued me.[7] Black feminism isn't a dogma with tenets every good feminist has to adhere to on pain of expulsion. There are as many ways to be a black feminist as to be a person, and the fact other black feminists disagree with some of Beyoncé's positions demonstrates how rich black feminism is with differences, contradictions, and productive tensions. As far as I'm concerned, the most important qualification for black feminist status is self-identification—a point made beautifully by journalist Janet Mock the day after Beyoncé branded herself a feminist at the 2014 Video Music Awards. "I applaud Beyoncé and her feminist stance, a declaration of her own independence as a leotard-wearing, butt cheek-baring, Blue Ivy-toting, equal pay advocating, Independent Woman-saluting, imperfect flawless feminist," she wrote in a post titled "How Beyoncé Pushed Me to Call Myself a Feminist." "I believe we waste much of our efforts policing one another—one of the many workings of patriarchy is to busy us with policing each other's choices rather than protecting them. Our duty is not to police feminists, our duty is to use feminism as a tool to check systems that uphold racism and slut shaming and sex worker erasure and anti-trans woman bias and general policing of other people's choices."[8]

The night Beyoncé stood up in front of a brightly lit sign that declared her a FEMINIST at the 2014 VMAs was transformational not only for Mock but for millions of black women. You could say Beyoncé's feminist self-declaration broke the internet—but you could also say the internet was temporarily fixed. Because for twenty years before that performance, the words most often associated with *feminist* were *militant, radical, man-hating*. But for two days after, the word most associated with *feminist* online was *Beyoncé*.[9] This means a generation of young women are growing up with something we've never seen before: an image of feminism that's overwhelmingly popular *and* undeniably black. And that's something *all* feminists should pay attention to. Janell Hobson rightly asks: "What, specifically, does this moment in popular culture mean for a younger generation of women who have been raised to be suspicious of feminism?"[10] Obviously, Beyoncé's popularization of the term *feminist* is in no way, shape, or form a solid enough foundation to build a next generation of black feminism on. Holding out *feminism* as something accessible for black women—a tool that can serve us, a light that can spark fires—is a beginning, not an end. Beyoncé has offered this word to a generation of black women and girls to claim, rework, and rethink in ways that work for us. This is the charge I give students on the first day of Beyoncé Feminism, and this is the charge I take on in this book: to use Beyoncé's music as a starting point to think through personal and political issues that matter in our lives as twenty-first-century black feminists.

But I'm writing about Beyoncé as not only a feminist but also a *femme*-inist. For over twenty years, I've lived my life as a lipsticked, high-heeled, glittery black femme—a "queer gender marked by a highly stylized and aestheticized" femininity, in the words of blogger Sublimefemme.[11] And for over twenty years, I've contended with folks suspicious of my feminism and my queerness alike. "Femme's intervention into heteropatriarchy has a history of being misread as yielding to heteropatriarchy's fantasy of femininity, but that is part of Femme's mystical glamour, its trickery," Sydney Fonteyn Lewis notes.[12] Misreadings like this—that assume "femmes [are] supposed to be lite; obsessed with clothes, hair and make up and treated like our primary purpose [is] to compliment butches"[13]—exemplify *femmephobia*: "the devaluation, fear and hatred of the feminine: of softness, nurturance, dependence, emotions, passivity, sensitivity, grace, innocence and the color pink."[14] Dismissals of Beyoncé's feminism routinely draw on femmephobia, too. Annie Lennox prided herself on rejecting feminine ideals and refusing to be "a dancing doll" in the infamous interview where she branded Beyoncé's stance "feminism lite,"[15] and Queen Bey's appearance on the May 2013 cover of feminist magazine *Ms.* elicited outrage at her hyperfeminine, sexy wardrobe. "On *Ms.*'s Facebook wall, numerous comments flooded the page in response to this cover, in which several *Ms.* readers left harsh, derogatory comments: from calling the pop star a 'fur-wearing stripper' and a 'whore' to discrediting her feminism," Hobson summarizes.[16] Yet no amount of feminist-shaming is enough to interest Beyoncé in covering her legs, reducing her bling, or diminishing her extensions, and her luxurious embrace of black femininity— even, *especially* when that femininity is dismissed as frivolous, retrograde, and insufficiently black feminist—is the primer that smoothes and binds the foundation of my Beyoncé femme-inism.

Beyoncé's triumphant, blinged-out persona visualizes for me that "not only is the Black and feminine an ancient identity of strength, power, and divinity," as Kaila Adia Story writes, "the contemporary manifestations of a Black femme identity are based on a Black feminist tradition of recovering and resistance that seeks to undermine the racist and heteronormative assumptions that choose to see femininity as inherently White, and power as inherently male."[17] Brushing through Beyoncé's *oeuvre* as a palette where I blend together black feminism, black femininity, and black femme-ness, I come to *Lemonade* hoping to elaborate what Lewis calls black femme-inist criticism: a set of critical reading practices that "investigate the ways that black women's cultural productions critique white heteropatriarchal construction of black women's race, gender, and sexuality."[18] Lewis's understanding of black femme-ness began with her rapturous engagement with popular culture images. "My particular articulation of femme resulted from my interaction with pop culture and the black femme images, which I found in the lithe frame of Josephine

Baker, the climatic whispers of Donna Summer, the uncontrollable curls of Diana Ross, the rasp of Billie Holiday, and the poetics of Toni Morrison, Nella Larsen, and Zora Neale Hurston," she recounts. "These images provided sustenance for my culturally malnourished queer of color spirit."[19] When she entered graduate school to theorize *something* about black femme-ness, Lewis faced a glaring gap in black feminist and queer studies. While black butches and transmen were beginning to theorize transmasculinities, black femme scholars rarely centered our own queer genders in our work. "The key to deciphering this 'something' was not to be found in mainstream feminist or queer theory: in fact, the black Femme remains largely invisible in both domains," she rightly observes. "I turn, then, to culture as a site from which to launch a black femme-inist critique."[20]

I've reread Lewis's essay, "'Everything I know about Being Femme I Learned from *Sula*,' or Toward a Black Femme-inist Criticism," many times. Each time, her lush, self-loving prose makes me wonder: why didn't I—as a graduate student or assistant professor or even a new associate professor of black queer studies—ever move to theorize my own black queer gender? Why did I never try to fill in a scholarly gap that gaped as wide when Lewis was a graduate student as when Matt and I met as PhD students? The answer isn't pretty. Although I never put this into words, my internalized femmephobia let me assume the queer gender I went to great effort to embody just wasn't interesting or important enough to write about. It wasn't until I reached the edge of forty that I was able to recognize—*I'm a grown woman, I can write whatever I want to* (to paraphrase Queen Bey). I've written away from internalized racism through black feminism, I've written away from internalized homophobia through black queer studies, and now I'm writing away from my tired, Reagan-era internalized femmephobia through black femme-inist criticism. I'm going to write about Beyoncé's girliness in the girliest way I know how here, embracing drama, beauty, pleasure, emotion, and the color purple. I'm also going to enjoy myself in the writing, sinking in to appreciating Beyoncé's sexiness and my own. Because I'm with Lewis when she declares black femme-inist criticism should be "sexy," should recognize desire as a means of "challenging critical regimes which demand separation of mind and body for intellectual rigor."[21]

My black femme-inist reading is also a reparative reading, in the sense explored by Eve Sedgwick in "Paranoid Reading and Reparative Reading, or, You're So Paranoid You Probably Think This Essay Is About You." I write this book in a moment of hyper-broadcast black death, when, as Austin YouTube vlogger Evelyn Ngugi puts it, "every reblog, retweet, repost of citizen video footage that ultimately will never see the light of a courtroom, every Vine you watch of someone you know from Twitter getting pepper sprayed, and every link to a racist GoFundMe page . . . takes a toll" on black women viewers in the US South.[22] The paucity of images of black Southern women's *lives* in popular media could easily inspire what Sedgwick calls *paranoid* readings: critiques that register resistance to dominant media images by following "academic protocols like maintaining critical distance, outsmarting (and other forms of one-upmanship), refusing to be surprised (or if you are, not letting on), believing the hierarchy, becoming boss."[23] A *reparative* reading practice, in contrast, fights to extract sustenance from a popular culture largely uninterested in the survival of marginalized—including black and queer—communities. Though so often dismissed as "sappy, aestheticizing, defensive, anti-intellectual or reactionary that it's no wonder few critics are willing to describe their acquaintance with such motives," the reparative reading is "no less acute than a paranoid position, no less realistic, no less attached to a project of survival, and neither less nor more delusional nor fantasmatic."[24]

A paranoid reading of *Lemonade* could easily catalogue limitations to Beyoncé's vision of black femme-ininity even as it bemoans violence toward real-life black cis- and trans-femmes eclipsed by her work. But my reparative reading looks to piece together fragmented images of black femme power in *Lemonade* to create images of black/queer/women's wholeness from whatever (admittedly flawed) cultural objects I have available. As much as I love Beyoncé and want to believe rumors about her affairs with Rita Ora and other women celebrities, ideally my black femme-inist criticism would focus on the internationally recognized cultural production of a self-identified black queer femme like myself. But while a few white cisfemmes—Portia de Rossi, Cynthia Nixon, Sarah Paulson—and black masculine-of-center folk assigned female at birth—Angel Haze, Young MA, Robin Roberts—have achieved celebrity in recent years, the same can't be said for black cisfemmes or other cisfemmes of color; which, Femme on a Mission writes, "is both a statement on the lack of diversity in the celebrity sphere in general, as well as in the celebrity gay community."[25] So, taking those lemons and making honey-sweetened lemonade, I'm extracting sustenance from the popular culture I share with black women around me. Like Lewis watching Donna Summer and Diana Ross, I reflect on how *Lemonade* offers public space that visualizes possibilities for performing race, gender, sexuality, and region *black femme-ly*, in ways other mainstream representations currently don't. This is my #blackgirlmagic labor of "femme luv," as sister femme-inist scholar Ulrike Dahl calls it.[26]

When I share this labor of femme luv with cisgender and straight-identified feminist colleagues, I sometimes receive the solidarity-minded suggestion I shouldn't "stop" with a femme-inist reading of Beyoncé. What might be more radical, they encourage, is to claim Beyoncé's persona as queer, too. But labeling Beyoncé "queer" when she neither claims that title for herself nor includes herself in LGBT communities and/or politics—and, edgily fabulous and hyperfeminine or not, always publicly proclaims and celebrates straight wife-and-mother-ness—seems like a rhetorical gesture that elides important day-to-day realities of how sexuality and gender work. To sit at my computer and claim Beyoncé and collaborator Big Freedia (discussed in chapter 6) are both queer levels the differences between black women who live with (always tenuous) straight privilege and queer-identified individuals like Freedia, whose gender and sexuality put her at daily risk of discrimination, incarceration, and premature death. As someone who moves with straight privilege in some situations but not in others, I'm keenly aware how real those differences are. While I'm not interested in claiming Beyoncé for "team queer" (until she does decide to leave Jay for me, of course), then, I *am* deeply committed to looking at how self-identified straight and queer femininities are coconstituted. That is, the way I want to blur lines between black femininities and black femme-ininities is by showing that Beyoncé—or any ideal of black womanhood—doesn't have to carry the label "queer" to be intimately related to black femme self-expression. The Texas Bama woman and the Texas Bama femme can dance in formation as fine-ass sisters, ladies, not twins; Beyoncé's lemonade can be sweet to me even if her recipe isn't the same as mine.

FEMME-ONADE MIXTAPE

Blue lipstick, bamboo earrings, sculpture platforms, faux fur, Bantu knot-outs: writing this book like a black femme means I wrote it while wearing all these things, sometimes. It means my body and my experience are blended into *Beyoncé in Formation* like highlighter—something not necessary to the textual makeover that is black femme-inist criticism, maybe, but part of the palette available to work with.

Blending lines between memoir and study, first and third person, subjective and objective becomes a tool for writing against black femme invisibility. "Like Laura Harris who, in her essay 'Queer Black Feminism: The Pleasure Principle,' supplements critical theory with personal narrative in order to write herself 'into history, by writing [herself] a history,'" Lewis writes, "I model a Black Femme-inist critical approach by weaving the personal and the theoretical."[27] When I write, talk, and teach in this way, people often reflect on my (apparently surprising) comfort with making myself vulnerable in my work. But my choice to write the way I do isn't about comfort—it's about a commitment to undermining femmephobia, which discourages feminine subjects from writing ourselves into our work by insisting that our self-expression reads as being soft, messy, over-the-top, or provocative. As my femme friend and mentor Ann Cvetkovich writes, "The femme who allows herself to be vulnerable removes the layer of toughness or the cortical shield that she might carry in the face of a homophobic culture that declares her desires to be shameful or does not recognize the beauty of her queer femininity."[28]

Bamboo earrings, sculpture platforms, Bantu knot-outs, Ankara prints, brass bangles, flower tattoos: writing this book like a black femme also means sidestepping linear narratives to twist, curl, and spiral like hair fresh out of a Bantu knot, rippling curves and circles everywhere. The chapters are written in vignettes that flow circularly in and out of each another, bringing Beyoncé into conversation with singers, actors, dancers, authors, activists, reality television personae, and plain old folks in my life. Of course, someone could write beautifully about *Lemonade* in a much more straightforward way—moving chronologically through music history from the blues to Beyoncé, maybe, or track-by-track through the visual album from "Pray You Catch Me" to "Formation." But writing in curlicues performs what my gorgeous femme colleague Juana

Rodriguez calls a *queer gesture*. The opening sentences of her book *Sexual Futures, Queer Gestures, and Other Latina Longings* describes the writing that follows as "an amorous gesture" that is "sexual in the queerest of ways, meant to inspire intense feeling rather than reproduction; it is multisensory, asynchronic, polysemous, perverse, and full of promise."[29] And while (following her suggestion) I in no way attempt to reproduce Juana's powerful writerly style, her femme-inist methodology inspires my own amorous gesture in the form of an "asynchronic, polysemous, perverse" text that sashays, circles, twists, and sidesteps its way toward Beyoncé in ways that are indirect, circular, and erotic.

Much as I love her, though, Beyoncé isn't my target audience here. Instead, *Beyoncé in Formation* composes a textual mixtape dedicated to all the women and femmes who listen to Beyoncé while we try to make fem(me)inist sense of our lives. In *Country Fried Soul: Adventures in Dirty South Hip Hop*, DJ and music journalist Tamara Palmer draws on both her musical and writerly skill set to write a "mixtape in book form"— and, like me, finds it a lot harder than she'd first imagined. "It made good sense at first. As a matter of fact, it seemed like the perfect approach for a book that aimed to open a window onto the world of the Dirty South by sampling of different voices and topics related to the music and culture," Palmer explains. "So what could be a better way of creating my first book, especially one as music and DJ-centric as this? The simple answer is anything else. Why? Well, I forgot one really vital thing about making mixtapes: It's fucking difficult."[30] Yes, readers, it is. Even though (like the ballerina I once trained to be) I try to make it look effortless, delving into so many fields outside my training—ethnomusicology, urban anthropology, sociology, new media studies, Southern studies, religious studies, art history—made this book challenging to write. Weaving all these disparate threads together might sometimes make *Beyoncé in Formation* challenging to read, too.

And while difficulty isn't my goal, it's also not something I shy away from: because understanding black women's art and lives *is* difficult, and when readers have to tie together a barrage of topics, histories, and ways of knowing in a single space—well, they do the same work that black women do every day to navigate our worlds. But, as Palmer puts it, "so long as everyone understands that what you hold in your hands is more a lovingly sampladelic oral history than a linear academic textbook about the Dirty South, no feelings should be hurt."[31] And understand this uneven mixtape, too, is an amorous gesture: that, as the 2017 Program Committee of the American Studies Association puts it, "the form of the mixtape itself—the compilation, the sharing of which is a sign and a producer of intimacy"—is a labor of black femme love.[32]

My *Femme-onade* mixtape plays in three parts. Each is comprised of twin chapters that explore black women's sexuality and gender in complementary ways, and each remixes the explorations of sexuality and gender that came before— so part 1 is remixed in part 2, which is remixed in part 3. Part 1, "Family Album: Making *Lemonade* Out of Marriage, Motherhood, and Southern Tradition," turns to Beyoncé's "Don't Hurt Yourself" to think through black feminist critiques of marriage, then complements this with a consideration of black feminist models of motherhood—as a gender in addition to familial role—in "Daddy Lessons." Part 2, "'Most Bomb Pussy': Toward a Black Feminist Pleasure Politics," moves beyond the traditional (marital) sexualities explored in part 1 to consider the black feminist uses of pleasure politics in "6 Inch"; and moves beyond considerations of traditional (heterosexual, reproductive) femininities to meditate on black Southern iterations of femme in "Sorry." Part 3, "Calling for

Freedom: Black Women's Activism in the US South" pushes considerations of sexuality into the political realm, viewing "Freedom" in conversation with movements for black women's reproductive justice; it expands the discussion of gender into contemporary LGBT politics as it celebrates the internet-breaking video "Formation," whose featured artist Big Freedia—rhythming the song with her declaration "I came to slay"—underscores why Beyoncé's black femme-inism isn't only for cis women.

When Matt and I met, I was in the first year of a PhD program in comparative literature where my focus was Caribbean women's writing in French, Dutch, and English. Which is to say—*nothing* in my formal training prepared me to do such a thing as write a textual femme mixtape about a pop megastar. But in the last seven years I've pushed myself out of my comfort zone in ways I never imagined: out of my relationship comfort zone by getting married, out of my geographic comfort zone by moving to Texas, out of my professional comfort zone by teaching and writing as a Beyoncé femme-inist. So here's my invitation to you as you read this: step out of your comfort zone, too, experiment with a way to remix your tried-and-true readerly practices. Sing the lyrics as you read them, try on a new shade of lipstick that matches the text (especially you, gentlemen), call your mother to ask a question about your grandparents, look up a reference that makes no sense to you, put aside your judgment about what counts as "serious," start a new hashtag, take this book to a protest, let your lover give you a foot rub while you thumb chapter 3. Why not? For the space of these pages, enter into the world of a Texas Bama femme: someone who lives between very real places in the South and the boundless territory of the black feminist imagination, someone who performs her womanness very diligently and very irreverently, someone whose life is nothing like Beyoncé's and everything like her complicated fantasy of blackness, womanness, and desire. This *Femme-onade* mixtape is for you, to make your own black feminist sense of—and maybe enjoy a little along the way, too. Oui chères, oui.

Family Album

MAKING *LEMONADE* OUT OF MARRIAGE, MOTHERHOOD, AND SOUTHERN TRADITION

My Femme-onade *mixtape opens with an old-school family album. An album that mixes together snippets of my family history, that lovingly collects stories and spills tea about the black ancestors and black imperfections excised from our memories since my grandparents left the South. And an album that travels through* Lemonade *to excavate the family history of musical genres like blues, rock, and country, reverently incorporating the black women those genres now gloss over or disavow. My album experiments with making black feminist sense of these literal and figurative family relationships, embracing the messiness of black sexuality and black womanhood that leaks outside traditional family stories. My Granddaddy Alabama, Grandma Louisiana, you mix that . . .*

QUEEN BEE BLUES

Steely blue-grays hold Beyoncé up and hover in the background, her cornrowed head and fur-coated body leaning against a wheelless gray vehicle trapped in a fluorescent-lit, graffitied, murkily sea-green garage. This is the image that began and ended the one-minute trailer HBO released on April 17, 2016, for *Lemonade*, "A World Premiere Event Next Saturday 9 ET/6 PT."[1] "The past and the present merge to meet us here," Beyoncé's voiceover opens in the empty blue garage, then continues asking: "What are you hiding?," "Why can't you see me?," "What am I doing, my love?"[2] Her excited viewers were left with even more questions. What WAS *Lemonade*? Friends, students, and Twitter speculated with me. An autobiographical film, like the *Life Is But a Dream* documentary she released on HBO in 2013? A narrative film, a music-driven sister to *American Horror Story* peopled with eerie shots that looked like a horror pic waiting to happen? Like every other self-respecting member of the Beyhive, I set my DVR to find out.

And when I tuned into HBO there it was in its lush, disturbing, unapologetic Afrocentric Southern gothic glory, a twelve-track visual album *and* narrative film held together by Warshan Sire's script of angry black feminist poetry. Divided into chapters titled "Intuition," "Denial," "Anger," "Apathy," "Emptiness," "Accountability," "Reformation," "Forgiveness," "Resurrection," "Hope," and "Redemption," *Lemonade* told the story of a woman who calls her cheating husband to task before ultimately giving their marriage another chance.[3] Now, lots of folks watched this hour-long protest against a black woman's betrayal and took it as an elaborately styled musical autobiography. Orli Matlow called

Lemonade "a raw, real confession about Jay-Z's infidelity"[4] and Cultured Creole named it a "heartbreak biography,"[5] while Leah Rocketto became one of many Twitter users who was "90% sure #LEMONADE is Beyonce's way of announcing her divorce."[6] Some fans were happy to see Jay Z get a public comeuppance—needling he "got 99 problems and . . . Queen B is all of emmm"[7]—while others mourned Beyoncé's postmortem of what many fans had admired as an exemplary black marriage. "If Beyonce got cheated on," Maria@cakefacedcutie summed up the moral of *Lemonade*'s story, "NO ONE is safe."[8]

But I saw something else, something that wasn't simple autobiography at all. By the time *Lemonade* got to its third song, "Don't Hurt Yourself"—the video the trailer's steely, angry-sad images were taken from—I was sure I was watching a filmic, twenty-first-century version of classic Southern black women's blues. Yes, there were musical nods. The song features blues-rock megastar Jack White and samples Led Zeppelin's "When the Levee Breaks," a twelve-bar blues authored and originally performed by classic blueswoman Memphis Minnie in 1929. What really resonated with me, though, were the ways I heard Beyoncé taking up classic blues themes. In classic blues, trifling men have long been metonyms for a patriarchy that never affords black women the love and life they deserve. Artists like Bessie Smith and Ma Rainey, Angela Davis tells us in *Blues Legacies and Black Feminism*, performed songs about lovers' broken promises as metaphors for the unfulfilled promises of freedom. Marriage and sexual partnerships have *never* fared well in black women's blues songs, but this isn't because black men aren't good husband material. "There are important historical reasons that romanticized images of marriage—and the permanency in personal relationships implied by this social institution—are absent from women's blues," Davis points out. "Normative representations of marriage as the defining goal of women's lives blatantly contradicted black social realities," she reminds us, and blueswomen's gutsy breakup anthems broke down prevailing ideals of wife-and-motherhood by "asserting their right to be respected not as appendages or victims of men but as truly independent human beings."[9] When Beyoncé throws her ring at the camera in "Don't Hurt Yourself," isn't she doing the same thing?

Like many Queen Bey devotees I fell in love with her music singing to her 2003 debut solo album *Dangerously in Love* and its breakout hit "Crazy in Love," featuring her then-boyfriend Jay Z. Dressed all in black and posed in a gangsta lean, Jay bends down to set fire to a line of gasoline that blows up a car parked under Los Angeles's Fourth Street bridge. Brilliant in the flames' orange light, Beyoncé saunters in with a chinchilla slung low on her shoulders to spin in front of Jay, flipping her loose hair and pressing her body to his, then dances into a backbend hanging off his side and playfully bats him with her stole.[10] The opening of "Don't Hurt Yourself" eerily echoes this scene—but recast from warm-lit romance to discolored horror film. Here, too, lines of gasoline are lit into flames around parked cars, but nothing blows up (the mood fiery, not masculine bravado–level destructive). Beyoncé leans against an unharmed vehicle wearing another chinchilla, tosses her now tightly braided hair to the sample of "When the Levee Breaks" and—pulling her fur tighter instead of letting it part suggestively—saunters in front of the SUV to reveal a black woman reclining on the hood and another sitting by the back wheel. This time *she's* walking with the gangsta lean, *she's* monochrome in her Yeezy gray sports bra and leggings, *she's* flanked by admiring sisters as she approaches the camera and, looming above the lens, challenges: "Who the fuck do you think I is? You ain't married to no average bitch boy."[11]

In MTV's "Making of the Video: Crazy in Love," twenty-one-year-old Beyoncé explains that video's romantic premise:

"[It] celebrates the evolution of a woman. It is about a girl who is at the point of a relationship. She realizes that she is in love, she is doing stuff she would not normally do but . . . she is just crazy in love."[12] All grown up, Beyoncé's character in "Don't Hurt Yourself" isn't on the point of a relationship any more—she's *questioning the point* of her long-term relationship. She sings the steely disappointment of marriage that follows love's first shiny promises, the long days and nights of being married when a black woman feels taken for granted like an "average bitch" and being "crazy" isn't so cute any more. Incinerating the tired myth that marrying a black man offers black women ultimate fulfillment, this chinchilla-wearing diva flips the script: she surrounds herself with women who appreciate *her* instead of performing bending-over-backward appreciation for her man, walks tall on six-inch heels instead of hanging on Jay like an appendage. And most importantly, she doesn't let her husband define her. No, she comes to tell us "who the fuck . . . I is" is her *own* damn self.

Welcome to the Queen Bee Blues.

* * *

When you hear about my reservations about marriage and see me excited about Queen Bey knocking down marriage ideals in her Hood by Air fur coat, please don't think I was raised with "bad" ideas about matrimony. Just the opposite. I grew up idolizing my mother's father John, who drove his Volkswagen camper from Massachusetts to California every June to see me and my siblings and brought balloons, animal crackers, and rose-colored stories of his marriage. John Talmadge Stapler was born July 25, 1919, in Birmingham, Alabama, the second of four children born to scraping-to-get-by George and Arties Stapler (the great-grandmother who came to me in a dream to tell me to get married before I moved South). When John was a baby Edith Wilson recorded "Birmingham Blues": *I know my man is waiting, my heart is palpitating / Back back back to Birmingham, in Alabam, Alabam.*[13] John Talmadge was never as nostalgic about Birmingham as all that. He grew up by North Birmingham railroad tracks listening to the blues and living the impoverished deep Southern life that inspired them, and before he made it out of segregated elementary school he knew he wanted his life to be an *anti*-blues. He didn't want to be the down-and-out lover left behind, didn't want to be the sweet man who left a trail of disrespected women in his wake. So stories of his stable, happy marriage are stories of his success, stories of his freedom from expectations, stories that prove he was a good man.

He *was* a good man, and to my grandmother he was the best husband in the world. A captain in the black army corps— who made the next-to-last cut for the Tuskegee Airmen—he was stationed in Offenbach, West Germany, after World War II when he met eighteen-year-old Herta. He promised her love, the sun, and the moon and she took them, until she got pregnant. Then the army transferred John to France and when friends warned her she'd never see him again, numbers were on their side. About five thousand "brown babies" were born to black servicemen in Germany after World War II and thousands, with fathers under pressure from army policies against "fraternization" and German mothers unable to provide for stigmatized black children, ended up in orphanages.[14] In October 1948, when my mother was eighteen months old and being called "nigger" on the playground, *Ebony* ran a cover with a black German boy that implored: "Homes Needed for 10,000 Brown Orphans."[15] But John and Herta defied the odds. John came back to Offenbach leave after leave until finally, when their second daughter was born, the army granted John's request to marry and legitimize their children Helen and Patricia. He gave a fictitious address in Chicago so he and Herta could wed, and John sailed across the Atlantic with his wife and daughters to start their life together stateside. The Staplers lived together as man and wife, so crazy in love I almost never saw them apart, until the day John died from a heart attack suffered while Herta was sleeping by his side.

It's an amazing story. Because I loved my grandfather so much, I grew up wanting to live in that story: dreamed of having someone love me so hard they'd follow me around the world, too, and that would be how I'd know I was a good black woman like he was a good black man. So there was a stream of girlfriends I implored to show their love by moving in with me immediately, whose difficulties with cutting back on tequila, finding a better job, or sticking to their decisions I thought I could make better with my all-conquering love. My friends from graduate school (including Matt) will tell you, and you can imagine, it was a disaster every time. Now, my grandmother is a strong-minded, self-respecting, fiery woman, and I know if my grandfather ever did her wrong she would have come at him strong with a German-inflected version of "you ain't married to no average bitch, boy." So I don't want a literal "Don't Hurt Yourself" story of my grandfather's life to follow up on the "Crazy in Love" fantasy of his marriage. But where are the stories of when life was messy, love wasn't returned, folks didn't treat you right, you mucked up again, *and you're still a good person?* The stories that let me know you that *wifey* status doesn't equal a woman's worth, and that I could still be a queen-worthy black woman without a mate to stand as living proof? If he didn't have those stories of his own or didn't want to share them with a little girl, well then, made-up stories would have been just fine. Just something to let me know that no matter how perfect a good black woman I tried to become, no one can ever—as Bey sings in "Hold Up"—be "too perfect / To ever feel this worthless" like you do when love doesn't work out.[16] Stories to gently whisper that being hurt, messy, and insufficiently loved can bring growth, opening, and their own kind of beauty, too. Or did my grandfather try to pass along all those messages, and I was just too young and literal-minded to hear them?

* * *

"Don't hurt yourself," Beyoncé sings dryly as she lifts herself up off the broken vehicle, repeating the first line twice like a classic twelve-bar blues. The irony, though—this song only exists because the singer and addressee have already hurt themselves, badly, by staying in a relationship where one partner was cheating and lying about it. Riding on a musical mashup of guitar-thrashing rock and Southern hip hop, the song's husband-confronting lyrics give us a *blues experience*: "an encounter with life, with its trials and tribulations, its bruises and abuses—but not without benefit of the melody and rhythm of song," as James Cone writes.[17] Beyoncé takes a lesson from musical grandmothers and spins a story of marital betrayal (real? fictional? does it matter?) into a chance to declare that black women like her want more, deserve more, can do more than the broken-down cars, men, and patriarchy she's expected to lean on. Maybe Beyoncé was cheated on and maybe she wasn't—but for certain she takes a story of personal betrayal as an opportunity to sing the blues for so many ways black women are vulnerable to hurt. As my research assistant Candice Lyons insightfully wrote to me about this song, "Beyoncé's experience of real-life interpersonal betrayal may have prompted her to think deeply about all of the myriad ways she and Black women in general are betrayed by the people and institutions they (we) try to make homes out of."[18]

After Beyoncé reminds her listener she's "no average bitch," she taunts: "You can watch my fat ass twist, boy / As I bounce to the next dick, boy." And she flips her fur coat up in back to punctuate her dig. Long-suffering wife-and-mother no more, Beyoncé refuses to lay back crying or twisting in the wind—she's twisting on "to the next dick, boy," that *next* sounding like she's lining them up. The addressee wants sex with multiple partners and no commitment? Beyoncé will take some of that too. When "papa likes his outside women, mama likes her outside men," as Ma Rainey sang in "Barrelhouse Blues."[19] These declarations of black women's entitlement to outside sex aren't just about pleasure-seeking (though sex for the sake of feeling good is nice, too). When blues depicts "a good time 'mama' no less at ease with her body and her sexuality than her 'papa,'" Davis writes, it "celebrates women's desire for alcohol and good times and their prerogative as the [sexual] equals of men."[20] Queer blueswomen like Ma Rainey and Bessie Smith weren't shy about advertising their lovers both male and female, Davis reminds us. And when Bey announces her planned infidelity with a lingerie-clad woman curled on the hood and another open-legged against the wall, the video teases the possibility the dick/dildo she's bouncing onto "must've been women / 'Cause I don't like no men" (to signify on Ma Rainey's "Prove It on Me Blues").[21]

Think the addressee's heard the last of Beyoncé's post-betrayal plans for her ass? Oh no. The opening lyrics come back, sharpened, in the second prechorus: "Hey baby, who the fuck do you think I is / . . . Just give my fat ass a big kiss, boy / Tonight I'm fucking up all your shit, boy." Beyoncé leans into the camera so hard she bumps it out of focus in the first line, then recenters to blow kisses at the lens with the force of slaps. The deserted, peeling-painted, flickeringly lit garage reads like a horror scene where violence could jump from the shadows at any time, and these lyrics suggest that time is coming soon for the addressee. The words themselves are violent, snatching back the "hey baby" of street harassment and flanking it with profanity—a shift from the PG lyrics of

Bey's premarital cheating songs like "Irreplaceable." "'Dirty words' are traditionally for the use of men only," Paul and Beth Garon write of blueswomen's profanity. "By treating such words as part of the male domain, women are divested of a significant amount of power, but men's power to abuse women with these words is mitigated and diffused by women's use of the same words."[22] And Bey promises something worse will follow her "bad" words. "Tonight I'm fucking up all your shit, boy!" Prowling the empty parking lot like lions, she and her crew have *what*, exactly, in store? Maybe a revenge fantasy like Bessie Smith's "Hateful Blues": "If I see him I'm gon' beat him, gon' kick and bite him, too / Gonna take my weddin' butcher gonna cut him two in two."[23] Sucking teeth at ideals of passive femininity, blueswomen have never been coy about fighting whoever wrongs them. "This rough-and-tumble, sexually aware woman is capable of issuing intimidating threats to men who have mistreated her, and she is more than willing to follow through on them," Davis admires. "She is a spiritual descendant of Harriet Tubman, who, it is said, always warned her passengers on the Underground Railroad that no one would be permitted to turn back, that they would all forge onward or die at her hands."[24] Hip hop routinely sings praises for the ever-loyal "ride-or-die chick," and Queen Bey lets us know she expects a ride-or-die man too. *Or else.*

Soon after her wedding, Beyoncé shot a 1950s-themed video for "Why Don't You Love Me" (2008) where her character B. B. Homemaker—distraught that her partner doesn't love her enough—shuts herself in a bedroom drinking martinis, smoking, crying mascara down her face, and yelling into the phone in distress.[25] The protagonist of "Don't Hurt Yourself" struts out a completely different vision of a black woman scorned, dragging her grievances into public space usually coded unsafe for women—the car park—and defiantly taking up space with her girls. Tearless and perfectly mascaraed as she announces "a bigger smile on my face being alone," Queen Bey walks triumphantly toward the camera with arms open overhead and legs akimbo, her body spread to its widest and boldest like an X. She looks good, too: the camera makes sure to catch her bouncing breasts barely contained by the Yeezy sports bra and lyrics call attention to her "fat ass," all that curviness wrapped in custom fur. This self-loving fierceness may be the most striking blues experience Beyoncé gives us in "Don't Hurt Yourself." While the "overwhelming majority" of Bessie Smith's "songs allude to rejection, abuse, desertion, and unfaithful lovers, the preponderant emotional stance of the singer protagonist . . . is far from resignation and despair," Davis reminds us, and the Empress of the Blues also sang about betrayal decked in furs, feathers, and pearls that defied stereotypes of black womanhood's abjection.[26] Love gone wrong, Bessie and Bey model, is neither a failure nor an end. No, ladies, it becomes an opening as wide as a body spread to its fullest, an opportunity for black women to manifest power, grit, and full fabulousness for the world to see.

* * *

At their first recording session on June 18, 1929, Memphis Minnie and Kansas Joe recorded "When the Levee Breaks"—a blues classic later reworked by British rockers Led Zeppelin on *Led Zeppelin IV* (1971) and sampled by artists as diverse as the Beastie Boys, Dr. Dre, Björk, and Beyoncé. The day of their second recording session, February 20, 1930, Kansas Joe McCoy and Minnie Douglas married in Shelby County, Tennessee. Minnie was a beauty who favored frilly dresses, high heels, silver jewelry, and flawless makeup, and fans came to see the Louisiana-born, Tennessee-raised singer, guitarist, and songwriter for her looks and talent alike. A publicity photo taken near the time of her marriage shows her smiling at the

camera wearing dramatic dark lipstick and a crown of flowers, her long chiffon dress slit almost to the waist to reveal a
slender right leg supporting her guitar. Fellow blues guitarist
Brewer Phillips remembers: "They had to fight the mens away
from her. She was, pretty hair, soft hair black, she could fix it
any way she want to; and boy, she used to look good. She kept
herself up, she's always neat, and the mens . . ."[27]

Oh, the mens. Rebelling against decorous wife-and-
motherness long before Beyoncé was a twinkle in her mother's
eye, Minnie was never coy about being a sexually adventurous
woman. When she ran away to Memphis as a teen she worked
as a streetwalker and throughout her career was known to bed
fellow recording artists for their share of the profits or "throw
[her] guitar down and turn a trick with somebody for three,
four dollars."[28] She had her share of nontransactional sex
partners before Kansas Joe, too, including bluesmen Fiddlin'
Joe Martin, Blind John Davis, Homesick James, and Peter
Chatman Sr. Her reportedly jealous husband left Minnie after
six years of musical and marital partnership. Minnie didn't
bother to write a single blues about that breakup, though,
and quickly moved on to another city—Chicago—and other
men. Stories remember she not only liked people to look at
her fine clothes, she liked folks to look *up* them. Studs Terkel
remarked that "the only thing about Memphis Minnie, she
pulls her dress so high when she come in and set up," and
one fan recalls she "liked for men to look up under her dress,
and she had on nice underclothes."[29] But "the mens" had to
be careful not to be fooled by her flowery dresses and lacy
underwear. Minnie was a "hell-cat" who had little patience
for unsolicited advances and could fight as well as she could
fuck. Johnny Shines admired, "Any men fool with her she'd
go for them right away. She didn't take no foolishness off
them. Guitar, pocket-knife, pistol, anything she get her hand
on she'd use it."[30] Femininity and fighting went hand in hand

in Minnie's expression of blues womanhood, and she made sure men knew she was their equal in jumping from bed to bed as well as fight to fight.

Minnie was a superlative musician whose varied skills as guitarist, singer, and songwriter defied gendered divisions of labor in the classic blues, but her musical legacy remains underrecognized. Just before *Lemonade*'s release Jas Obrecht profiled nine great blues guitarists of the 1920s and '30s in *Early Blues: The First Stars of Blues Guitar*, and not one was a woman; several of Minnie's lovers made the collection, but not Minnie herself.[31] Yet at a time when women were expected to shine only as vocalists, Minnie played and fingerpicked guitar better than most bluesmen. "Minnie's role as a female country blues guitarist (and later as an urban one) helped shatter . . . stereotypes of gender-based role performance," Paul Garon declares. "Minnie was the lead guitarist in all of her partnerships and has been hailed as a skilled guitarist with few equals."[32] Minnie was also a prolific songwriter, whose lyrics combined sexy double entendres ("I got a bumble bee, don't sting nobody but me" her best-selling "Bumble Bee" begins)[33] with themes of Southern country life. "When the Levee Breaks," her sister-in-law Ethel Douglas believes, was based on her experience in the Great Flood of 1927. "The levee *did* break, and we left from there. I'm sure that's what she was singing about in 'When the Levee Broke' 'cause we were scared to death when it broke."[34] But the song isn't autobiographical: written for Kansas Joe to sing, it tells the story of a man who works unsuccessfully to fortify the levee before leaving his flood-wrecked home and lover. And in the tradition of lover-left-me blues, it refuses to descend into a story of defeat. "The blues is a technique of psychic mastery," the Garons reflect. "*When the Levee Breaks* was not a cry of pain but an announcement of a new beginning, even in its sadness."[35] Maybe Minnie's artistry in turning lemons into lemonade—as well as turning guitars into weapons and sex into power—is what inspired Beyoncé to salute her legacy in "Don't Hurt Yourself." "Oh crying won't help you, prayin' won't do no good," the lyrics of "When the Levee Breaks" advise.[36] God helps blueswomen who help themselves.

* * *

Just after Beyoncé spreads her body into a fur-coated X, she taunts the trifling addressee: "Motivate yourself, call me Malcolm X." With these words the music stops abruptly and images of the parking garage disappear. Close-ups of black women on New Orleans streets flash across the screen as audio of Malcolm X intones: "The most disrespected person in America is the black woman. The most unprotected person in America is the black woman. The most neglected person in America is the black woman." This speech, given in 1962 at the funeral of a black Muslim killed by police, goes on to proclaim "the only time a Muslim gets real violent is when someone goes to molest his woman. We will kill you for our women, I'm making it plain, yes, we will kill you for our women."[37] Racist "molestation" is only one of the overlapping forms of male violence black women face, though. In *Arrested Justice: Black Women, Violence, and America's Prison Nation*, Beth Richie devastatingly details a "matrix of violence" that leaves black women at risk for simultaneous physical, sexual, and emotional violence from partners, communities, and the state—and confronting just one of these will never liberate the black woman from her position as the most "disrespected . . . unprotected . . . neglected person in America."[38] Who protects black women disrespected by our husbands, Beyoncé asks? Chronically dismissed as "men being men," the "emotional abuse and stress inherent in dealing with infidelity" remains underestimated, Ebony Utley suggests.[39] An interviewee in her study of black wives and infidelity explains why marital betrayal cuts deeper than stranger assault: "It's not just, oh, you've taken my heart. No, to me it's deeper than that, it's like, it's almost like you've carried this person in your womb. You've allowed him in all these years and then for him to take something that was most precious to you and disrespect it and misuse it is like . . . it was just very very deep."[40] Parking lots are dangerous places for women, sometimes; sometimes marriages are too.

But Beyoncé sharpens the trope of the injured wife by reminding the addressee of Malcolm's deeper point: a black man who doesn't value black women ultimately *hurts himself*, because he doesn't value himself. "When you hurt me, you hurt yourself / Try not to hurt yourself / . . . When you love me, you love yourself / Love God herself," Bey sings with Jack White. Their lyrics echo the questions that began Malcolm X's speech: "Who taught you to hate yourself from the top of your head to the soles of your feet? Who taught you to hate your own kind? . . . You should ask yourself who taught you to hate being what God made you." The black man will never be fully human, he inveighs, until he loves every part of himself *unconditionally*—including "his" women, whom he must protect with the same fierceness white men protect their wives and sisters. Hortense Spillers offers a similar, but resolutely feminist insight in her classic essay "Mama's Baby, Papa's Maybe." Misogynoir harms not only black women but black men, she argues, because it dehumanizes the black mothers we all come from. For black men to rehumanize themselves, they need to value not (just) black manhood but black womanhood: "it is the heritage of the mother that the African-American male must regain as an aspect of his own personhood—the power of 'yes' to the 'female' within."[41] Or, as Beyoncé lances in the outro to "Don't Hurt Yourself": "You know I give you life."

The first time I watched *Lemonade*, the moment Malcolm X's voice shut down "Don't Hurt Yourself" was the moment I *knew* I was listening to the blues. When the car park reappeared on screen, it looked to me like a twenty-first-century version of the alley Memphis Minnie sings about in "Down in the Alley": "You got me in the alley, but don't get rough / I ain't gonna put up with that doggone stuff."[42] Now, the alley is more than an alley here—it's a metaphor for the shadowy social space where black women stay disrespected, unprotected, and neglected. Minnie addresses an individual *you* to make her listeners pay attention, yes, but the roughness she's calling out is collective: the brutality of black women's unfreedom in an America where intersecting oppressions try to keep our lives as narrow and unlit as an alley. "The lyrics of women's blues . . . explore frustrations associated with love and sexuality and emphasize the simultaneously individual and collective nature of personal relationships," Davis puts forth. "In blues discourse generally, the personal relationship stands both for itself and for unrealizable social aspirations and failed dreams."[43] Blueswomen never took that social failure without protest. They sang their own power to make change: "Can't see no light / Got to feel my way out this alley / Gonna stop, boys, walking late at night," Minnie declares. And Beyoncé's feeling her way out, too. "If you try this shit again, you'll lose your wife," she warns, and throws her wedding ring at the camera to punctuate her threat. That's right—wifey's on her way out and an angry black feminist's here to take her place, demanding overdue love like "God herself."

* * *

My grandfather was twenty-seven years old when he arrived in Germany having already led a full young man's life in Birmingham. The first in our family to attend college, he graduated from Miles College with a degree in English. In 2006, my mother and I flew to Birmingham and visited Miles. We asked the college archivist for help locating documents pertaining to my grandfather's time there, and she posed basic questions to direct our search. What year did he first enroll? Which church did he attend? What were the names of his college sweethearts? Because my grandfather told so few stories of himself, we didn't know the answer to any of these questions—but the last one haunted me most of all. Having heard so much about his life-changing love for my grandmother, it quite simply never occurred to me that he had girlfriends before her. And that in segregated Alabama those girlfriends would have been black women, his churchmates or classmates or barmates. (My cousin told me he was a drinker when he was young.) Immediately I wanted those other stories. Because of course, everyone wants to know they came into this world through a great love. But if you're a black woman—disrespected, unprotected, neglected—you also want to know you come from ancestors who loved black women deeply, since the wider American world never has. Out of respect for his wife, my grandfather never told those other stories. But as his oldest black granddaughter, I needed stories of his love for black women to know women like me were deeply, life-changingly loveable in his eyes, too. I still need them, even if I have to invent them for myself.

* * *

Memphis Minnie began her recording career just months before the stock market crash abruptly ended the champagne days of classic blues. The opulent fur coats, free-flowing liquor, and well-paid women artists of the roaring twenties gave way to down-and-out, guitar-picking, hard-living black blues*men* who became the voice of country blues during the Depression. While the class politics of this shift have been heralded as progressive, its gender politics were not. What "happened to the vaudeville blues women was not at all unusual," the Garons note. "To hire black men to fill jobs once held by black women was consistent with sexist practices of the day and upheld the mainstream cultural notions that a woman's place was in the home, that men were better than women at most jobs, and it was a man's role to work for a living for the rest of 'his' family."[44] The downturn of Bessie Smith's career in the 1930s is emblematic of how women artists were sidelined. Columbia paid her $200 per usable side for recording at the height of her career, but by the 1930s that amount was reduced to $37.50—while the label hired numerous male stars like Peg Leg Howell or Barbecue Bob for $15 per side. Minnie probably received a similar amount for "When the Levee Breaks," and the Garons observe: "It's doubly ironic that Minnie, who was so often said to 'play like a man,' was also *paid like a man* in this atypical case where women were paid more than men."[45]

The blues inspired hybrid genres like rhythm and blues in the 1940s and blues-rock in the 1960s. But while black musicians dominated the former, white British rockers like Led Zeppelin, Eric Clapton, and the Rolling Stones shot to superstardom in the latter. Earning millions and accolades with their arrangements of black Southern blues like "When the Levee Breaks," these rockers often spoke reverently of country bluesmen, but they seldom credited women blues artists (let alone black women rock musicians like Tina Turner). Though the genre's popularity waned after the 1970s, the turn of the millennium saw a blues-rock revival in Britain and the United States. At the forefront of this revival: Beyoncé's "Don't Hurt Yourself" collaborator Jack White. The Detroit native and his wife Meg, who formed the pared-down blues-rock group the

White Stripes, rose to prominence in UK and US garage rock scenes with the release of their third album, *White Blood Cells* (2002). Even as Jack's guitar prowess was deeply inspired by country bluesmen Charlie Patton and Blind Willie Tell, he self-consciously designed the White Stripes' pop-art aesthetics and Coca Cola–inspired signature colors to distance their blues from black forefathers. "All the aesthetics about the band and the way we presented them was a great way to get away with playing the blues," he told *Total Guitar*. "People wouldn't notice that I was this white kid born in the 70s playing the blues because they're wondering why we were wearing black, white and red."[46]

Beyoncé hasn't publicly told the story of how she came to collaborate with Jack—Jay Z's business partner in the Tidal streaming service—but Jack gave his version on NPR's *All Things Considered*. "You know, I just talked to her and she said, I wanna be in a band with you," he laughed. "I've always loved her voice—I mean, I think she has the kind of soul singing voice of the days of Betty Davis or Aretha Franklin. She took just sort of a sketch of a lyrical outline and turned it into the most bodacious, vicious, incredible song . . . 'Don't Hurt Yourself' is incredibly intense; I'm so amazed at what she did with it."[47] Brittany Spanos, in her incisive *Rolling Stone* piece "How Beyoncé's 'Lemonade' Reclaims Rock's Black Female Legacy," suggests a more complicated take on White's collaboration. "Beyoncé's choice to not only work with White, a forerunner of the movement to bring back blues-rock in the new millennium, as well as sample Led Zeppelin's 'When the Levee Breaks,' which was itself a reworked version of a song by black Delta blues artists Kansas Joe McCoy and Memphis Minnie, is a shrewd statement on the genre's complex lineage," she appreciates. "She re-appropriates a hard-rock version of a blues classic that gained more traction and recognition than the original, while teaming up with the new standard bearer for the intermingling of blues and rock."[48] Spanos comes out strong when she asserts: "Seen in this light, the fierce and vengeful tone of 'Don't Hurt Yourself' takes on a broader cultural meaning."[49] The easiest interpretation of this song is that Beyoncé's singing *with* Jack *to* her cheating husband. But what if she's singing *with* and *to* Jack—not the individual, but the representative of contemporary blues-rock that builds on black women's legacy without giving us acknowledgment, appreciation, or love? Then her guttural threats—"Just give my fat ass a big kiss boy / Tonight I'm fucking up all your shit boy"—become another kind of black feminist artistic protest. As Candice Lyons drives home, "It's also relevant, I would think, that the person who delivers the line 'Love God Herself' is always White, which perhaps points to a musical acknowledgment that 1) God is a Black woman and 2) for White to love Beyoncé specifically and Black women generally is for him to ultimately love what gives him (and his career) life."[50]

Right after these lines, the chorus returns. While the first chorus was Jack's solo, Beyoncé interrupts him mid-line to force a duet in the second. "When you hurt me . . ." Jack begins and Beyoncé finishes angrily: "*You hurt yourself.* Try not to hurt yourself." As she does, the diva runs toward the camera pointing an accusing finger then holds up her left hand to signal *stop*. Yes, stop, the Queen Bee Blues commands, *just stop* what you're doing to black women. If you think marriage is a black woman's ultimate fulfillment, you're lying to yourself. If you think black women are going to take disrespect from husbands, strangers, or America itself lying down, you diss yourself. If you think black women are going to let ourselves be pushed out of the legacies we've sewn, you play yourself. So stop underestimating black women, because you do so at your own peril. We're here to fight hard as rock(s) for the love, justice, and recognition we deserve—and you just better try not to hurt yourself.

* * *

Everyone in my family agrees my husband looks a lot like my grandfather. He does, and these men share a lot of wonderful qualities. Both have distinctive, rolling laughs. Both think the sun rises and sets in their wives' eyes. They both grew up seeing women mistreated and have no tolerance for men who cheat on, lie to, or raise even a voice to lovers and wives. And both came from deep poverty they escaped through education. I remember two stories my grandfather told me about his life before my grandmother, and their common moral was the importance of education. One was a laughing memory of hiding under the bed in his mother's small house to do school assignments in peace and quiet. The other was a cautionary tale about the year he was supposed to go to fourth grade but had to take a full-time job in a grocery store after his father died. The first day of school the following year, he put on his delivery boy's outfit to go to work and his mother beat his behind. She had no intention of letting him drop out of school permanently, she let him know, and he'd better get ready to go to class with his brothers and sister.

When I was a girl and a teenager, my grandmother spoke to me often about the importance of the man I'd marry and how to choose a good one. But my grandfather never talked about love, marriage, or motherhood as part of my future. Instead he encouraged my studies, practiced French with me, told me to work hard in math and science because that was how to get ahead in the world. It's not every black girl who grows up with a grandfather who firmly believes she can be a chemist, nuclear physicist, or rocket scientist, and I appreciate his certainty I could do anything. I wonder, now, if his silence on the topic of marriage meant more than I understood at the time. If that was my grandfather's way of seeing and communicating that wife-and-motherhood was never going to define who I am, never going to be the one and only story I told of my life. He died before I graduated college, but maybe he already foresaw what would come to pass—that I'd have many years coming into my own as an intellectual and an academic before I was in a place to have a daughter first, then a husband second.

When I was three and four years old, my grandparents came to visit me bearing blue Mickey Mouse balloons. They chose blue—not the pink most little girls got—because it was my favorite color, and they sometimes treated me to blue cotton candy too. Blue is still my favorite color, so I know how very many shades it comes in: baby, sky, powder, peacock, turquoise, navy, steel, indigo, midnight. Since she has a daughter by the same name I like to think blue is Beyoncé's favorite color, too. "The world is blue at its edges and in its depths," she quoted Rebecca Solnit's *A Field Guide to Getting Lost* on Tumblr soon after her daughter's birth. "The purer the water the deeper the blue. The sky is blue for the same reason, but blue at the horizon, the blue of the land that seems to be dissolving into the sky, is a deeper, dreamier, melancholy blue, the blue at the farthest reaches of the places where you see for miles, the blue of the distance. . . . The light that gets lost, gives us the beauty of the world, so much of which is in the color blue."[51] And if there's one thing I've learned from following the Queen Bee Blues from "Don't Hurt Yourself" to Memphis Minnie by way of Angela Davis, it's that the blues comes in as many shades, textures, and forms as there are experiences in people's lives.

He never told me this himself, but years after he died my mother disclosed the other story my grandfather hoped to be able to pass down: the tale of how he came to earn a PhD in chemistry. After he retired from active military duty he worked as an army chemist, earning a master's degree by taking night classes, then asked for time off to pursue a PhD. But the lab

Herta Post and John Talmadge Stapler on their wedding day.
Courtesy of Helen Tinsley-Jones.

where he worked denied his request, although they'd granted
the same request for white colleagues. His dream as a boy who
idolized George Washington Carver had been to grow up, get
a PhD, become a professor—but instead the great story of
his life was a more tender one, the love of a wife and children
who made faraway places feel like home. My dream as a girl
was to grow up and fall hopelessly into love that would last
forever—but instead I became the PhD, the black feminist
professor whose life's work is to imagine a world where black
women are valued as much as we deserve. In the end, no life
can be an anti-blues but no life can always be a blues, either.
"Believe it or not, even the president has the blues," blueswoman Koko Taylor once said.[52] Your blues ain't like mine,
Grandpa John, but I hope you're proud of me still. Any story
we tell of wanting more than we have, loving more than we're
allowed, and refusing hurt without protest, well, that's a beautifully blue story.

MAMA SAID SHOOT

On November 2, 2016, the 50th Annual Country Music Association Awards broadcast live from the Bridgestone Arena in Nashville, Tennessee. After two hours of country music history–themed acts hosted by Carrie Underwood and Brad Paisley, the moment the Beyhive was waiting for arrived. The gold-lit, "CMA"-emblazoned curtain lifted to reveal Beyoncé and the Dixie Chicks flanked by a stage full of black musicians dressed in white and white musicians dressed in black, clapping Beyoncé and Dixie Chicks lead singer Natalie Maines into the opening lines of "Daddy Lessons." "Texas," Beyoncé crooned, and Natalie answered "*Texas,*" calling together their shared home state. The audience was on its feet for their rendition of "Daddy Lessons," which the Chicks began covering on their comeback tour days after *Lemonade*'s release. The collaboration was country music history in the making: Beyoncé's first CMA appearance and the Dixie Chicks' first since Natalie's controversial 2003 remarks about fellow Texan George Bush and the Iraq War. And it was certainly one of the show's standout moments. "In typical Beyoncé fashion, she led a regiment, filling the stage for a backyard-barbecue that became a Bourbon Street parade with a fabulous sax solo in the bridge," Spencer Kornhaber noted in the *Atlantic*. "It also stood out for another reason: She and her musicians were some of the only black people at a ceremony celebrating an art-form whose origins, as is well documented, were nowhere near entirely white."[1]

"Beyonce and Dixie Chicks performing together is my personal proof that I serve a God who answers prayers," one tweet enthused.[2] But not everyone was so appreciative. "Why are you showing Beyoncé & Dixie Chicks? One doesn't believe in America & our police force while the other didn't support our President & veterans during war," a Facebook user demanded, and another quipped: "Neither are country, and Beyoncé could not be bothered to put some clothes on for the occasion."[3] (She wore a sheer floor-length dress.) Some artists attending the show shared similar reservations. Alan Jackson left his front row seat when the performance began and Travis Tritt launched a Twitter rant against Beyoncé the next day. "Apparently, the CMA thinks Beyonce is as relevant to country music as Loretta Lynn, Tammy Wynette or Patsy Cline," he huffed, adding, "I'll tell you why! Because the CMA folks don't think country music is strong enough to stand on its own."[4] Bey's supporters responded in full force, decrying the implicit—and too often, explicit—racism embedded in outcries against Beyoncé's countryness. One user shot back, "Ppl mad Beyoncé performing at the #CMAs but forget that black folks invented country music,"[5] and *Rolling Stone* writer Andrea Grimes lanced: "But here's how fragile whiteness is. We can't even acknowledge the existence of a country song performed by a Black woman."[6]

The vitriol that met Beyoncé's CMA appearance was not only racist. Misogynoir also discolored viewers' reactions—which, like the Facebook post above, were often laced with slut shaming. "Disgusting! This is someone's wife, this is a mother! And just look at it! Nasty satanic skank," one commenter exclaimed, while another judged: "What a nasty dress to wear in front of all the little children who will see this, devilish whore."[7] When I re-viewed the CMA performance to teach "Daddy Lessons" in February 2017—just before Valentine's Day, just after Beyoncé's pregnancy announcement—I realized this controversial gown was, in fact, a maternity dress: the belly it half-exposes must already have been growing twins Rumi and Sir in November. Taking the stage in a see-through version of Loretta Lynn's signature floor-length, puff-sleeved gown, Beyoncé both evokes and flouts "country's prevailing image of valued femininity: the sentimental mother, who embodied home, domesticity, and a lost rural past."[8] Alan Jackson, who fled when Beyoncé took the stage, exemplifies this devout, self-abnegating country mother in "Home," which praises his Mama Ruth as a woman who "found her strength in faith of God / And a love of family / She never had a social life / Home was all she knew / Except the time she took a job / To pay a bill or two."[9] But instead of styling herself as a black version of this sentimental mother to appeal to country fans, Beyoncé sang with three other Texan mamas about learning to shoot like *fathers*: "Daddy made a soldier out of me," Beyoncé crooned in the first verse and the Dixie Chicks chorused, "Oh, my daddy said shoot." When Natalie soloed on the second verse, Queen Bey, who (maybe because of her pregnancy) left out her signature choreography that night, couldn't resist turning around to shake her ass as Natalie sang, "My daddy said shoot . . ." As if Blue Ivy's mother was giving anyone who didn't like her see-through dress a chance to kiss her black ass, while Natalie warned they'd come to shoot haters down.

For every hater who trolled the web after the show, though, more country fans and artists came out in support of Beyoncé. Chris Stapleton, 2015 CMA winner for male vocalist, best new artist, and album of the year, was among the stars who came to Beyoncé's defense: "She's everything you want her to be. She's a classy, classy lady, and I'm proud that she could take the time to come show up."[10] Thank you, Mr. Stapleton. But did Beyoncé *have* to be a "lady" to belong at the CMAs? No matter how poor she is, the sentimental mother of country music is, of course, always ladylike—passive, patient, chaste, selfless, hard-working, and pious. But in "real life," all kinds of country mothers populate the South: sharecroppers and moonshiners, cowgirls and conjure women, baby mamas and backwoods abortionists. Where are songs to praise *them*? If

Beyoncé and Natalie aren't "good enough" to represent country motherhood, what does that mean for all the colorful, messy, hard-loving women who're too busy making life possible for their children to act like long-suffering, ever-forgiving, leg-crossing angels?

Not only is the sentimental mother an impossible ideal for black women to live up to: mamas, it's an ideal that's *not good for our daughters*. In her devastating study of black battered women, Beth Richie finds that black women who idealize their mothers are more likely to form abusive relationships—that emulating the "perseverance," "discipline," and "strong sense of morality" they admire in their strong black mothers leads them to stay with violent partners, believing real women are strong enough to "take it" and do the "right thing" by keeping fathers with their children.[11] Black women who avoid abusive partners, on the other hand, are the more realistic sisters who never put their mothers on pedestals they later hurt themselves trying to climb onto. Their childhood memories "were less glorified, and they did not recall feeling in awe about their mothers' personal qualities. They expressed a more accurate and specific awareness of and sensitivity to the social circumstances that typically limited their mothers' lives."[12] Mamas, you see, it's a good thing to be as transparent as Beyoncé's dress about the fact that we're only human: that sometimes we get fed up or lonely or jealous or crazy or horny or petty, just like daddies—or anyone else. And that imperfection is something to purposely pass on to our daughters, so sometimes, when they need to, they can just say *shoot*. Beyoncé's "Daddy Lessons" is also an opportunity for us to think about gender lessons.

* * *

"Beyoncé may have made headlines with her performance at last night's Country Music Association Awards," Julia

Brucculieri wrote the morning after the show, "but not even Queen B could steal the spotlight from the one and only, Dolly Parton. The country music icon was one of the night's biggest honorees, taking home the Willie Nelson Lifetime Achievement Award."[13] Stellar women artists including Reba McEntire, Carrie Underwood, Martina McBride, and Jennifer Nettles serenaded Dolly with her own songs, moving her almost to tears. "Thanks to all these beautiful girlfriends of mine," Dolly beamed as she accepted the award. "I just want to thank all my fans and everybody for letting my little girl dreams come true."[14]

I'm going to confess something that won't surprise anybody: before watching this awards ceremony, I didn't know much about country music. But since Beyoncé, Natalie, Dolly, and her beautiful girlfriends held me spellbound that night, I've collected the autobiographies of several country singers who piqued my interest—including Dolly's *My Life And Other Unfinished Business* and her sister Stella's *Tell It, Sister, Tell It*. From my minicollection of women country singers' autobiographies (something this black feminist never expected to own), I've learned a bit about the ideal country mother. Dolly credits her capacity to dream to mother Avie Lee, who she remembers "planting a bunch of dreams and watering them with sweat and tears."[15] Reflecting on her vision of Avie Lee's motherhood, Dolly is the first to admit: "People have often said that we put Mama up on a pedestal, to which I always reply, 'Shoot, that was the only way we could keep Daddy away from her!'"[16] Dolly's father never stayed away for long: Avie Lee gave birth to twelve children and survived one near-fatal miscarriage before a doctor removed her uterus after her youngest daughter's birth. Despite the fact she traveled with one child in her belly and another on her hip most of her adult life, Avie Lee, Dolly remembers, was a tireless worker who spent every waking moment doing for her children. After making family dinner out of whatever she could muster, she stayed up quilting by the light of a kerosene lamp as her children listened to her tell Bible stories. In her song "Mama," Dolly reveres her as "The one that never sleeps 'til all's in bed / The one that never eats 'til all are fed / Her never-ending love / Her gentle, caring touch / She never asked for much / Mama."[17]

But can a mother so perfect exist anywhere but in a song? Dolly's sister and fellow country singer Stella remembers their mother's life less rosily. Not so quick to put Avie Lee on a pedestal, Dolly's little sister places her in a sickbed: she remembers their mother frequently confined to bed or hospitalized while she, Stella, took care of her siblings. "My mother was creative when she wasn't ill, which wasn't too often," Stella recalls. "I've come to realize, she suffered from postpartum depression almost all the time from being pregnant. If she wasn't sick and pregnant, she was suffering with depression after having had the last baby. . . . What a life for her! And what a life for her children!"[18] When Stella was seven, her sister Willadeene married and Dolly went to live with an aunt. Stella, the next oldest daughter, was "in the second grade when I became mainly responsible for the entire household of eight people until I left home at fifteen . . . I did most of the cooking, cleaning, laundry, and childcare. I felt abandoned by my two older sisters. I never knew a time I did not feel responsible for others."[19] Stella's own song about Avie Lee, "Up in the Holler," is laced with the loneliness of being the parentified child of this sick mother: "Up in the holler / Where the birds and the whippoorwill sing / Oh I sometimes get so lonely / To hear those childhood things."[20]

Both sisters understood the challenges Avie Lee faced as a teen bride with no health care, education, or steady income, and both saw her burdens as motivation to create "better" lives for themselves. Their aspirations to a more privileged womanhood crystallize in their fascination with makeup, a luxury Avie Lee never indulged in. "Womanhood was a difficult thing to get a grip on in those hills, unless you were a man," Dolly writes with her trademark wit. "My sisters and I used to cling desperately to anything halfway feminine. . . . We used to love when our aunts would come to visit. They had been out of the mountains, even to other states, and they knew so much. . . . They had purses filled with lipstick and powder and eyeliner and all kinds of things we had no access to. This was the real ammunition in the battle of the sexes."[21] That ammunition, she imagined, could protect her from repeating Avie Lee's lack of control over her body—from girlhoods and womanhoods where "men and boys could just put their hands on [girls] any time they felt like it, and with any degree of roughness they chose."[22] Stella—who recounts her attempted rape by a congressman while in full stage makeup—is clear that women aren't protected from male violence either by makeup or by the class privilege it represents. But makeup and the benefits of independent womanhood do something else for her. When she learns her father had outside children while married to Avie Lee, Stella sends her half-sister Laura "some makeup in a caboodle box with a note"—a gesture recognizing their shared Parton womanness.[23] Just as Stella pens a more realistic view of their mother than Dolly does, she suggests a more realistic vision of what relative privilege can offer women. It can't protect us from violence in this patriarchal world we live in, no, but it can help us create connections with one another. *Tell it, sister.*

* * *

The day after her CMA debut, Beyoncé released "Daddy Lessons" as a stand-alone video. *Lemonade*'s longest video release to date, this Tidal exclusive opens with a three-and-a-half-minute sketch titled "Accountability." The camera dollies out from a still, breezeless bayou, then cuts to a garden view from the balcony of a plantation great house, centering a blonde black girl as she walks down a brick path to the door. Interior shots move viewers through "women's spaces"— bedrooms, nursery, dining room—and people the master's house with playful black girls. Abundant with antique furniture, lace, crystal, fresh flowers, and domestic happiness, the opening is an idealized scene of black girl- and motherhood where girls dress dolls, jump on four-poster beds, chase each other downstairs, and watch their beautiful mother—an off-center Beyoncé—perform her toilette. Beyoncé's voiceover describes a daughter's discovery of this mother's lipstick: "You find the black tube inside her beauty case where she keeps your father's old prison letters. You desperately want to look like her. You look nothing like your mother. You look everything like your mother. Film star beauty."[24] But—like the slave quarters visible behind the garden as the blonde girl comes up the path—a hint of disquiet shows through this home scene as the narrator advises: "You go to the bathroom to apply your mother's lipstick. Somewhere no one can find you. You must wear it like she wears disappointment on her face." That disquiet is swept over as deftly as lipstick covers mother's lips, though, as the next line goes on to declare: "Your mother is a woman, and women like her cannot be contained." Loyal to an incarcerated husband, impossibly beautiful to her daughter, strong enough to create a sense of possibility from a life of disappointment: couldn't she be the sentimental mother of a country ballad?

But then "Accountability" cuts from this plantation fantasy to the contemporary streets of New Orleans, navigating through a rainy day in a poor black neighborhood. The film turns grainy, the camera moves more quickly and unsteadily, and the point of view falls to the eye level of a young girl. "Mother dearest, let me inherit the earth," Beyoncé's voiceover entreats as the video cuts to a little black girl shot through the slats of a fence, behind her the feet, legs, and drinks of trumpet-playing men who, from her perspective, look like giants. "Teach me how to make him beg. Let me make up for the years he made you wait," Bey intones as the girl smiles at the camera. A mother kissing her daughter's finger as she bandages it; a young black woman alone in a parking lot; a black girl covering her ears as adults fight around her; a close-up of another girl's unsmiling face against a concrete wall: these images flash across the screen as the narrator recounts a litany of abuses she suspects her mother has survived. "Did he bend your reflection? Did he make you forget your own name? Did he convince you he was a god? Did you get on your knees daily? Do his eyes close like doors? Are you a slave to the back of his head?" As desperately as the narrator wants to be like her mother, she's not too blinded by admiration to see that the ideal qualities of a country mama are the same qualities that make her vulnerable to abuse: that selfless devotion to wife-and-motherhood makes it easy to lose herself in wife-and-motherly duty, and that unquestioning faith in God the father sets her up to bow to her children's father as if he were God.

In the idealized, smoothly shot plantation scene, the lipstick representing picture-perfect motherhood is an ambivalent prize. It's something the mother—who's hidden it next to the father's prison letters, as if it reminds her of her own kind of incarceration—doesn't seem to want to pass on; something that looks like disappointment to the daughter who sneaks to wear it, but only where no one else can see. But when the camera turns to grainy, waterlogged, lonely, angry, hurt images of women and girls in New Orleans, these unvarnished snapshots of black mothers' lives illustrate the narrator's call to "inherit the earth." Stepping out of black-girl fantasy into complicated, painful black women's realities motivates this daughter to resist the patriarchal domination that made her mother "a slave to the back of his head," as she pledges to her mother and herself: "Let me make up for all the years he made you wait." And as Beyoncé's voiceover ends and horns lead into the song itself, "Accountability" asks viewers to look at how these on-screen patterns relate to our lives. "Am I talking about your husband or your father?" the narrative concludes pointedly. No, this last line makes clear, Beyoncé isn't confessing an individual situation—isn't (just) talking about her parents Tina Lawson and Mathew Knowles, but about *every* mother and father. And about all of us who are somebody's children, too. "Accountability" tells us we all need to develop "a more accurate and specific awareness of and sensitivity to the social circumstances that typically limited [our] mothers' lives," as Richie puts it, so we can try to change those circumstances instead of repeating them. So we can decide how and when we want to look *nothing like our mother* and how and when we want to look *everything like her,* too.

* * *

In honor of the CMA Awards' fiftieth anniversary, wife and husband stars Trisha Yearwood and Garth Brooks performed a medley of legendary country songs. Among these was a duet the couple had covered for years: "Louisiana Woman, Mississippi Man," originally recorded in 1973 by award-winning duo Conway Twitty and Loretta Lynn. Of course, no CMA retrospective could be complete without a tribute to Miss Loretta, the First Lady of Country Music. In 1972 she became the first woman to break into the country music boys' club by winning the industry's most prestigious award, CMA Entertainer of the Year. When Minnie Pearl jubilantly announced, "The Country Music Entertainer of the Year is: Loretta Lynn!" Loretta ran to the stage in a floor-length green dress and heels to greet a crowd cheering on their feet.[25] Four years later Loretta also became the first woman and second artist (after Johnny Cash) to publish a country music memoir, *Coal Miner's Daughter*, made into an Oscar-winning film in 1979. When I didn't know anything else about country music, trust, I knew Miss Loretta's music.

In 2002 Loretta published a follow-up memoir, *Still Woman Enough*. The preface frames the book through a conversation with twins Patsy and Peggy—the youngest of her six children—who asked why she wanted to write a second memoir when the first was a classic. Well, she replied, she left out a lot of the first book and the second would tell "*the rest of the story*"—including difficult parts of her fifty-year marriage to Oliver "Doolittle" Lynn that she hadn't written about when he was alive but now wanted to share to help women in similar situations.[26] So while the first memoir glossed over Loretta's struggles as a teen mother married to an alcoholic, the second paints a franker portrait of her rough-and-tumble experience of motherhood: one devoid of fantasies of long-suffering sentimental motherhood because she was too busy grappling with the realities of being both parents to her children. Married at thirteen, Loretta got pregnant a month later and Doo—frustrated with his bride's disinterest in sex—sent Loretta back to her parents' house. There, her mother decided it was time Loretta learned some facts of life she'd neglected to teach her: how to hunt and fish. "My daddy loved 'possum and trapped them, but Mommy was the hunter," she explains. "I learned to fish and hunt just like Doo and my mommy. . . . I was a good shot, too, and still am."[27] Knowing the traditionally husbandly skill of hunting was as crucial to Loretta's mothering as it had been for her own mommy. After reconciling, the Lynns moved to Washington State where Doo sometimes disappeared for weeks, leaving Loretta to provide for the children. During one of his absences Loretta and her babies were eating nothing but dandelion greens when she spotted a pheasant a hundred yards away. The only weapon she had was a .22 rifle whose stock Doo had broken in a moment of anger, but she managed to use it to kill the pheasant with a single shot. "I cleaned that bird, and it was the first meat the kids and me had in three weeks," she remembers proudly.[28]

Marriage and motherhood also taught Loretta the importance of fighting like a man. Doo was physically and verbally abusive to his wife, and the scenes of beatings he dealt Loretta in front of their children are some of the memoir's most difficult to read. But there are no stories in which Loretta is resigned to a beating by anyone. "I worry that people who read *Coal Miner's Daughter* or saw the movie think I am some helpless woman who couldn't, or wouldn't take up for myself. My foot! . . . I was often the one who threw the first punch."[29] She illustrates this with the story of a fight that happened when daughter Cissie was two months old. One night Doo promised to take Loretta out "for the first time in a long time" but stumbled through the door with a bottle of whiskey in his hand, announcing he was going back out. "That fired me up because I knew durn well he was on his way to see some woman," Loretta remembers. "I hauled off and hit him squarely on his mouth, knocking out his two front teeth."[30] None of Loretta's demands that he stop sleeping around and stay home with his children had ever worked before, but that blow managed to keep him temporarily faithful. "He looked so bad that he didn't take up with any other women until we had enough money to pay for his false teeth. And that was several months later. It tickled me half to death." Loretta tells this story to show not only her toughness but her imperfections, what she calls her "meanness": "I ain't proud of that story . . . but [it] has such a good ending I got to tell it anyway."[31]

By the time the twins came along, the dynamics of the Lynn marriage had changed for the better. Loretta was touring full-time and a gentler (though still drinking) Doo stayed home to care for the twins, gifted with the chance to tune into his own maternal side. Patsy and Peggy had no memories of the younger, raging, disappearing Doo until their mother shared them; while this was a motherly gift she knew it was difficult for her daughters to receive, she also understood it as a crucial one. Though Loretta never modeled for her daughters the possibility of leaving an abusive partner, she did model that it was in nobody's interest for women to conform to traditional gender roles when those roles didn't serve them—that they shouldn't sit quietly with hands folded when they needed to raise a gun or a fist to provide for their children or protect themselves. Being empowered to shake off so-called "feminine" passivity in this way is one of the hallmarks of women who avoid abusive partnerships, according to Richie. "The women in this subgroup reported that they did not temper their actions based on a sense that they needed to fit into a set gender role," she writes. "They felt that their behavior was less regulated by social or family expectation."[32] One of her interviewees explains: "I realized that the best way to get out of the house was to act like a boy, which meant doing boy-like things . . . not listening, fighting, breaking rules. . . . Oh, I liked pretty dresses and to go have my hair done, but I knew that would never get me anywhere."[33] So yes, Miss Loretta ran up to the stage to receive her Entertainer of the Year award wearing a floor-length, money-green dress and bouffant hairdo. But she got to that point in her life and career by being able to shoot and fight "just like my brothers," and now all her daughters know that.

* * *

"Texas. Texas. Texas." As horns lead into the opening lines of "Daddy Lessons," grainy shots of Beyoncé's native Houston intermingle with images of New Orleans: children walking together, young women laughing on a corner, a black man riding a horse down a city street with his daughter on the saddle in front of him. Threading these images together are two scenes that weave through the rest of the video: one of Beyoncé singing at Fort Macomb, another of her riding a horse through the Texas countryside. Now, spotting Beyoncé on horseback in her videos is nothing new. We've seen home movies of her riding as a girl in "I Was Here" (2011) and shots of her showing her power on a rearing black horse in "Run the World (Girls)" (2011). But the sheer Texanness of this version of Bey's horsewomanship—where the denim-clad, barefoot singer rides in front of a black man in a cowboy hat—impressed some viewers. "What really stuck out to me was Beyoncé riding a horse," columnist Michael Arceneaux admitted when asked what image of *Lemonade* stayed with him longest. "That might seem random to most, but if you're Houston, you are not a stranger to the sight of people—yes, Black people, too—riding horses down the street or on a sidewalk. Like many things she does, it reminded me of home. I love how committed she is to showing her Texas and Louisiana roots. . . . It always makes me happy to see the biggest star in the world be so damn country."[34]

Black Texans wear ten-gallon hats and bolo ties and ride horses in the street as part of a cowboy heritage that mainstream country music routinely overlooks. At the height of cattle-herding, Beyoncé's home state boasted the most black cowboys in the United States—one-third of all black cowherds in 1890 and two-thirds in 1910. Among these were many black cow*girls*, some as famous in their day as their male counterparts. Henrietta "Rittie" Williams Foster came to the Texas coast as a slave and worked as a cowgirl and midwife. "She liked to ride horses and it was said she was the only woman who worked with the men," her great-granddaughter recalls. "Wherever men were workin' cattle, she was workin' with them. She rode side-saddle and bareback on her white horse. She could ride like an Indian because she was half-Indian."[35] Black Seminole Johanna July, freeborn in Mexico, became a horsebreaker on the Texas border. "As a girl, Johanna was not required to do a woman's work about the place," Florence Angermiller learned when she interviewed Johanna at age seventy-seven. "Her meals were always ready for her and her clothes were washed. Her job was to break horses, take them to water, cut grass for them, look after the other stock and ride, ride, ride."[36] Just as Rittie and Johanna defied gender roles in their work, they bucked conventions around wife- and motherhood, too. Rittie used herbal contraception to limit her offspring to a single child, Lizzie: "She knew how to fix a woman so she couldn't have children. Aunt Rittie didn't want no children because she had seen women have such hard times, so she once told [Lizzie] she was real lucky to be here."[37] When Johanna found herself in an abusive marriage to a man who beat her for bungling housework, she got on her horse and rode off—then found two husbands who treated her better. As Beyoncé prays "Mother dearest, let me inherit the earth," it's the earth worked by these Texan foremothers that I imagine her inheriting: an earth whose herbs black women harvest to control their fertility, a landscape they navigate so skillfully they can outrun any man who pursues them.

Beyoncé is on horseback when she first sings the hook of "Daddy Lessons": "My daddy said shoot, oh my daddy said shoot."[38] The next lines explain this fatherly advice, which places Bey in the gun-wielding protector role usually reserved for oldest sons: "He taught me to be strong / He told me when I'm gone / Here's what you do / When trouble comes to town / And men like me come around / Oh my daddy said shoot." As Beyoncé trails the *oooo* of her first "shoot" she and her horse ride into the sun's glare, creating a momentary halo around her braid-crowned head. For this black mama, being angelic doesn't mean passively enduring the same kind of trouble her father gave her mother—it means, like the biblical angel Raguel, delivering wrath on men for "their sorceries or their sexual immorality or their thefts."[39] Beyoncé is also on horse-back for the final chorus of "daddy said shoot," and expertly sways down and to the right to avoid low-lying pecan branches as she sings "oh my daddy said . . ." Riding by nut-laden trees (with all their testicular symbolism) isn't a challenge for this Texan woman, who's tough as a pecan shell herself.

Henrietta Williams Foster, Johanna July, and Beyoncé's "Daddy Lessons" personae are all black country mothers. Not waiting, hoping, and praying like a sentimental mother, mothering for these women means fighting: mouthing off, making men beg, shooting when trouble comes to town, pro-tecting ourselves and our children by any means necessary. Because, y'all, sometimes a mama needs to talk as tough, shoot as straight, and ride as tall as any Texan cowboy. And that, too, as Michael Arceneaux puts it, is "so damn country. Said with love."

* * *

One of the reasons country women's autobiographies capti-vated me so hard is that in reading them I imagined a pic-ture of what life was like for my grandmother Fannie Jane. A lifelong country music fan, Fannie Jane was the daugh-ter of a sharecropper, like Dolly; and as a young mother she moved with her husband to rural Washington, like Loretta. She died of lung cancer before I was born—in 1967, the first year of the CMA awards. Fannie Jane was born in Pleasant Hill, Louisiana, the fifth of seven daughters and the fairest-skinned. Once they moved from Pleasant Hill, Fannie's family explained their brown-skinnedness as the mark of being "part Indian." But my father and his daughters think it's more likely in that part of Louisiana—where Indians were marched to Oklahoma long before Fannie was born but black folk still made up half the population—that the family's melanin came from African ancestry they weren't eager to claim after leaving the parish where everyone knew their family history. The parents, grandparents, and great-grandparents of Walter Gasche, Fannie's father, are easy to trace back to Germany and (New) England. But no one in my family has been able to find any information about Eva Davis, Fannie's mother and the parent whose dark skin made them "part Indian." Eva's birth year is listed on Fannie's birth certificate as 1890, and the only Eva Davis whose birth was recorded within ten years on either side of that date was a ten-year-old black girl who lived with her parents Lewis and Mary in Pointe Coupee Parish during the 1900 census. She disappears from the family home by the 1910 census, and while I can find later records of her sister Bessie, Eva evaporates from all records. Maybe because she married Walter Gasche, who moved with his wife from Pointe Coupee to Sabine Parish around that time.

Fannie Jane's parents left Louisiana for Iola, Kansas, when she was six, so the stories my father has of Pleasant Hill come from his Aunt Bessie (named after Eva's sister?)—who remembers accidentally chopping a toe off with an axe and being bitten by a rattlesnake there. Fannie Jane went to school through sixth grade in Iola and, five days after her twentieth birthday, married Howard Moran Tinsley. A picture of the newlyweds taken in November 1939 shows Fannie Jane beaming with her cheek pressed to her husband's, pencil-thin eyebrows framing limpid brown eyes, hair in fashionable side rolls (just a few baby hairs loose) to set off her heart-shaped face. She may not have known it, but Grandma Fannie was a mother-to-be in this picture: her first son, Howard, arrived eight months later. Fannie Jane went on to have six more children. My aunt El Tora, named after the El Toro cigars her husband loved; my father Jimmie; my aunt Morana, also named for her father; and my uncles Richard and Stephen arrived between 1942 and 1947. And then—just when it looked like she was done with pregnancy and childbirth—my grandmother had one more daughter, the only one she didn't name for her husband. Sweet Loretta, the baby girl.

My father was so grieved by his mother's early death that he never talked much about her until I asked. When I wondered in an email what made her happy, he wrote: "It is difficult for me to recall specific things that made my mother happy. I was the third of seven children, and I think her children were the primary source of her happiness. Her life while we were growing up was really invested primarily in us. Stephen was not quite twenty when she died, so she did not have much time to develop a life outside her children." When I followed up by asking what made her sad or angry, he responded: "I have a rather idealized image of my mother, and my memory is undoubtedly selective. I really don't remember her being angry. She would be upset at my father at times and would complain to me about him, but I don't remember it being with anger." I heard unspoken implications in his memory of Fannie's complaining to her children about her husband. With the exception of her oldest son, all Fannie's children have troubled childhood memories of Howard. In the stories I've heard, he only raised a hand to his wife once—a beating his namesake extracted her from. But his verbal and physical lashing of his children was consistent as the sunrise. If Grandma Fannie's children were her life, what did it mean to her to see Howard treat them like that? Was complaining about him her way of showing her children she was on their side? Howard gave Fannie seven children who made her life worth living— seven children she was proud of, seven children who passed for white, children who would have an easier way in the world than she did. Was that enough to make her happy? Did it make up for everything else? Did she ever think about leaving and if she did, what stopped her?

* * *

When I call Beyoncé's persona in "Daddy Lessons" a mother, it's not just because of the shots of her with a little girl in "Accountability." It's also because of two home videos that interrupt "Daddy Lessons" halfway through the second verse: one of Beyoncé on a couch with father Mathew when she was a girl, another of Mathew playing with Blue Ivy on a hotel bed. The video of Blue is inserted into the middle of the earlier video and has no sound of its own. Instead, little girl Beyoncé's voice speaks over the footage of her father and daughter laughing and jumping on a bed: "Have fun," she answers when Mathew asks what she wants to do with her grandparents, "have fun!" Blue's first appearance in *Lemonade* suggests Beyoncé is thinking about black women's relationship with their fathers not only because she's a daughter, but also because she's now a mother. Blue's home video folded into Beyoncé's shows a daughter repeating her mother's patterns with men; shows that however Beyoncé responded to her father in the past is set up to become the script Blue follows when she interacts with her grandfather, father, and all the men she loves.

When *Lemonade* premiered, Twitter launched plenty of jokes about what the album would mean to Blue Ivy when she's old enough to understand its subject matter. "'Hey, uh, dad?'—Blue Ivy after watching Lemonade in like 10 years," one user tweeted.[40] But Blue's cameo halfway through the sixth of twelve tracks—at the exact center, the heart of the album—suggests Blue's reaction to her mother's critique of marriage and motherhood is no afterthought. That yes, *Lemonade*'s portrait of a black woman's sadness, anger, and doubt is meant to show black girls that mothers have no place on pedestals, that mamas have complex lives and feelings too. But it also shows Blue that her mother doesn't suffer fools lightly—whether that fool is her husband or her father—and that no woman needs to. Despite the Twitterverse's jokes, that message may be one that protects Blue in "like 10 years." Richie finds that black women who avoid abusive relationships had mothers who were not only forthcoming about their own shortcomings but also brutally frank about those of the men in their lives. "This subgroup tended to identify with their mothers in more ways than African American battered women, including taking on their mothers' dismissal of or disdain for men," she explains. "Their mothers were less generous with their tolerance and more discounting of men's roles in their lives. In this way, they were significantly less vulnerable to men's violence as adults."[41] Beyoncé's daddy taught her to shoot when trouble comes to town, and now Blue's mother is teaching her daughter the same lesson. *Mama says shoot, oh my mama says shoot.* And on the album version of "Daddy Lessons," the track ends with Blue Ivy expressing her appreciation: "Good job, Bey!" she laughs, black girl to black girl.

* * *

By the time Loretta was out of diapers, my Grandma Fannie Jane's life had softened at the edges. Her older children were moving out of the house and getting their own jobs so family money went further, and as financial stresses ebbed Howard's temper flared less easily. Fannie Jane was able to do things for baby Loretta that she never could for her older children. Little Loretta had a curly-haired doll with eyes that opened and shut, a tricycle, and even a swing set. Loretta was born with a hole in her heart, a congenital birth defect, and when she was six she underwent a routine surgery to repair it. Loretta died on the operating table for reasons no one's ever been able to explain to me. Fannie Jane, devastated, buried the swing set along with Loretta so no other child could ever use it. She never recovered from her daughter's unexpected death and a few years later, followed Loretta to the long home of the ancestors. If my Grandma Fannie Jane was the perfect country mother my father remembers, a woman whose children were all she lived for, perfect mothering killed her: when her beloved child died she followed her, making sure that even in death Loretta would never be alone.

Even though I never met her, I've always felt close to my Grandma Fannie Jane. I call on her, talk to her, ask for her protection and guidance especially in everything around my own mothering. I know—I hope, really—she wasn't the ideal, self-sacrificing mother my father remembers. Even if it meant she was less perfect than her children remember, I wish she'd lived long enough so I could have seen her, climbed on her lap, played with her, learned from her in the flesh. Louisiana, Kansas, Washington, Texas, Tennessee: there's no place in the world for perfect mothers, no place such a woman can survive. All I want to have, all I want to be is a *real* mother and grandmother: flaws, heartbreak, lipstick, weapons, and all.

In July 2017, as I was writing this book, my father Jimmie flew to meet us in Austin so that he, Baía, and I could make the five-hour drive to Pleasant Hill to see Fannie Jane's birthplace. The town is so tiny that no hotels are closer than a half hour away, and to get a copy of Fannie's birth certificate we had to travel half an hour in the opposite direction to the parish seat of Many. While we were there I learned stories of my great-great-grandmother Elizabeth Delight who died birthing her twelfth child at age thirty-six and was buried in a Modoc cemetery near her husband's trading post; about my great-uncle Neely who went into the Navy during World War II and never came home; and, in true Southern style, about the real

Fannie Gasche and Howard Tinsley, 1939.
Courtesy of Howard Elija Anthony Tinsley.

first names of all the family members my father only knew by their nicknames or middle names until we went through government records. But try as I might, I never located any record that could tell me anything about Fannie Jane's mother Eva (whose name is Creolized as "Evoir" on Fannie's birth certificate) or any of her family members. No marriage certificate exists to show that Eva Davis and Walter Gasche were legally married, which of course they could not have been if she were of African descent. Eva Davis is a hole in our family tree and a hole in my heart. Great-grandmother Eva, did your mother miss you when you left? Did she know what became of you and the names of her granddaughters? What kind of mother was Mary Davis, and what stories would I have of her if you hadn't erased the blackness from your past in search of a "better" model wife-and-motherhood? Mary Davis, Mary Davis, Mary Davis.

"Most Bomb Pussy"

TOWARD A BLACK FEMINIST

PLEASURE POLITICS

Yes, my Femme-onade *mixtape started as a family affair, but now I'm going to play with something a little different. Something for those nights when you're with your girls, laughing in your living room or bedroom getting ready to go out or stay in together. For nights when you're enjoying each other's curves and angles and D'ussé and swag and the promise of that* good good *later. Because carving out space in our homes, our languages, our lives where we can push sexuality and womanhood into shapes that work for us—that's black feminist work, too. So let's talk about sex, Beyoncé fem(me)inists, and not just the marital, put-a-ring-on-it kind. Let's talk about how to make it creative, messy, profitable, hilarious; not just for women but for femmes, for those of us who wrap our legs around the legs of butches and femmes and transmen to hold on for the "most bomb pussy, because of whom sleep evaded." This is sexuality and fem(me)ininity for our generation of Southern black women.*

LOVE THE GRIND

Do you remember? Beyoncé's black python trench coat peek-a-booing a deep plunge La Perla bodysuit, thigh-high stockings, and sin-red Louboutin pumps as she strolls into the headlights of a Rolls Royce limo and climbs in back with Jay Z. "Now my mascara running, red lipstick smudged / Oh he so horny, yeah he want to fuck," she croons as Jay runs a hand between her lacy thighs in the backseat.[1] You *know* you remember, because how could you forget? *Beyoncé*'s "Partition" video was "so sexy," entertainment reporter Olivia Wilson swooned, "you'll want to have sex with it;"[2] so sexy, conservative pundit Bill O'Reilly fumed, it would inspire horny teenagers to make babies in backseats.[3] "Partition" may be the steamiest video on a visual album as hot as Texas in August, from its praise-song for cunnilingus ("Blow") to its D'ussé-soaked bathtub sex ("Drunk in Love") to its celebration of female ejaculation ("Rocket"). And lots of grown-ass black women like me said *yaaasss* to this black wife-and-mother getting that nasty, turnt up, squirty *good good* and not feeling bad about it. "Much has been made about how explicitly sexual this album is, but to me, it's one of its shining points," black feminist blogger Cate Young noted. "This album is sex positive in a very powerful way, and that's an important message for black women to receive. It's incredibly important that black women know that they do not have to shrink themselves or deny themselves access to pleasure in pursuit of respectability."[4]

Now, I was remembering "Partition" when *Lemonade* gave me a medium close-up of Beyoncé in the back of a limo, wide black hat covering her eyes and red light bathing her face and cleavage as she sings the first lines to "6 Inch": "Six-inch heels, she walked in the club like nobody's business. . . ."[5] *Hell yes,*

I thought, *here comes the sexy!* And I was right—but the sexy came different than in *Beyoncé*. In "Partition," Bey and Jay ride tangled in each other, oblivious to anything outside their luxury limo; but here Beyoncé, alone, peers at seedy streets with grate-enclosed windows, flashing signs for ATMs and cigarettes, and faceless men plodding by. And in "Partition," sex is no-holds-barred recreational, messy as scandal—"he Monica Lewinsky'ed all over my gown"; but in "6 Inch" sexiness is work, getting over without getting off. Beyoncé rides the limo to a peep show where "she work for the money from the start to the finish" and "don't gotta give it up 'cause she professional."[6] The red-lit ho stroll of "6 Inch" is a different world from the luxury ride of "Partition," a scene where sexiness has to provide something besides orgasms to be good—and if it's not good, Queen Bee's not having it. Angelica Bastién sums up the difference between this album's "sexiest song" and *Beyoncé*'s: "In her last album, Beyoncé was at her most sexually liberated. She dives even deeper into the topic in *Lemonade*, looking at it beyond simple lust and the ways a crumbling relationship can change the texture of sex. . . . This is Beyoncé at her most grown-woman level."[7]

Much as I love bejeweled Beyoncé from "Partition"—and you *know* I do—this red-lit Beyoncé offers edgier possibilities for imagining black feminist sexuality. Uncomfortable and imposing as six-inch heels, *Lemonade*'s vision of sexual power ditches glossy sex-positivity for *ratchet feminism*: a sexual politics born out of the creative ways "everyday Black women—including those who self identify as ratchet, thots, baby mamas, gold diggers, money-makers, bawse bitches, and haters" negotiate sex that *works for* them.[8] Straight out of black Louisiana, *ratchet* circulates in Dirty South hip hop as an insult leveled at black women seen as uneducated, hypersexual, gold-digging, confrontational, or tacky. But the word is reclaimed by feminists like Brittney Cooper, who embraces *ratchet* as a celebration of the unabashed sexuality, fierceness, and resilience of Southern working-class black women. With the Crunk Feminist Collective, Cooper imagines: "This new moment (not wave) in feminism represents the feminism of Sapphire's belligerent daughter smacking gum and rocking bamboo earrings, cherry-red lipstick, a Black Girls Rock! T-shirt, and some Js, while listening to Beyoncé's 'Flawless' on her iPod. Ratchet culture, accessorized with gold-plated grillz, spinner rims, and twerk tutorials, is the antithesis of respectability."[9] Prior to *Lemonade*, Beyoncé—a diva rumored to only have had sex with her husband, who Aisha Durham calls the "Southern belle of hip hop"[10]—floated above ratchetness in public opinion. But fed up with giving up wifely lap dances and blow jobs without getting what *she* wants, *Lemonade*'s narrator drives the ho stroll in search of how ratchetness can work for her—in search of how she can *get her own* without fear of being called pushy, thirsty, or slutty. Done cleaning up Lewinsky-esque messes, "she fights and she sweats those sleepless nights / But she don't mind, she loves the grind."[11] Love the grind, sisters, and love, the grind: the work, hustle, the daily same-old, the dance you do in six-inch heels.

All sex and all kinds of sexiness are transactional in one way or another. Martha Nussbaum points out we all "take money for the use of our bodies," and the labels black women get slapped with for our bodily work—*ratchet, ho, gold digger*—are "stigmatization . . . based on class prejudice or stereotypes of race or gender."[12] The wedding ring Beyoncé wears in "Partition" doesn't change the fact she's making money from (singing about) a blow job—and instead of stigmatizing her for that, what if we celebrated her using sexuality as an artistic medium and getting paid for it, too? If we need to admit all sex can be work, well, we also need to recognize all work can be creative, and L. H. Stallings pushes black feminists toward "analyzing what has been termed *sex work* through the immaterial of creativity and imagination, conceptualizing it as . art experience."[13] Driving into *Lemonade*'s narrative of marriage with red lights and peep shows, "6 Inch" opens space for us to see that marriage (or *any* relationship) shouldn't be the end of black women expecting to get *something real* for our sexiness. And that getting that *something* is its own kind of art—one that, like Beyoncé, we develop over the course of a sexual lifetime, cultivating the dancerly skill you need to slay in six-inch heels.

* * *

A nice middle-class black girl, I was raised to wear sensible shoes. My beautiful mother—who wore two-inch sling-back pumps to her wedding and owned no other heels—bought me a single pair of sturdy flats at the beginning of each school year, and I never owned heels until college. Now I have a walk-in closet lined with rows of stilettos, chunky heels, and platforms ranging from three to six-and-a-half inches, animal prints, spikes, and metallics brightening the space. My tennis shoes are platforms and my summer flip flops are, too, lifted five-and-a-half inches above the hot Texas pavement. Last time I wore them to a pedicure my nail technician appreciated them and told me, "If I didn't know what you do, I'd think you were a dancer, you know? A stripper."

My (semi) serious heel collection blossomed with the Beyoncé course. When UT first posted the course in October 2014, student newspapers, public radio, and Yahoo! News contacted me for interviews and *ABC News*, BuzzFeed, Madame Noire, and Clutch Magazine ran stories. Naively, I wasn't prepared for the buzz Queen Bey's name in a course title would cause. But when local NBC affiliate KXAN asked for a segment on the evening news, I *knew* what I needed to pull off a television appearance—so I bought gold stiletto ankle boots tall enough to feel powerful for the cameras. The segment was picked up by CNN, garnering happy congratulations from family, friends, and colleagues and hateration from trolls. "Professor Tinsley is an embarrassment to all women," one opined, and another commented: "If there hasn't been a level worse than degeneracy, I think we've just found it."[14] This low-key slut shaming made me feel *yes*, I must be doing *something* right—because "you know you that bitch when you cause all this conversation."[15]

The truth is, when my nail technician compared me to a stripper and the troll called me a "degenerate"—which I think is conservative Christian for "ho"—they were right. As a black feminist scholar hired by UT to talk, write, and teach about sexuality, I make my money off what I know about sex. Discussing her own use of her "pimp/ho degree (PhD)," sexuality scholar Stallings gives us this truth: "Historically and legislatively, writing, directing, and producing sexuality or representations of sexuality meant to arouse has been classified as a form of sex work."[16] No, I'm not being so disrespectful as to suggest the work I do at my computer and in the classroom compares to how prostitutes and strippers put their bodies on the line to earn money. But I am clear that my hustle as the PhD my grandfather always dreamed of is no better or worse than theirs. So if you want to call me *ratchet* for that, well, that's more than fine with me.

* * *

Beyoncé fem(me)inists, I absolutely adore that part of my job as a professional purveyor of black women's pleasure politics is surfborting through popular culture looking for the ways fierce black women and femmes lay claim to our unapologetic sexiness. And the April that *Lemonade* broke the internet, the blogosphere was rich with black feminist sexual self-expression—no small part of it taking up Beyoncé's vid-eos as a prop to ramp up our public sexiness. A week after *Lemonade* dropped, self-styled video vixen Karrine Steffans took to the blogs to remind everyone she gave Jay Z a back-seat blow job years before Beyoncé sang "Partition." "Over 15 years ago, I had Beyoncé's husband," she declared. "Yes, I was one of Jay Z's Beckys back in the year 2000 for about three minutes, which is about as long it takes me to satisfy a man in the back of a Maybach while overlooking the beaches of Malibu."[17]

Karrine had told this story before: her sexual thank you to Jay Z (who cast her in his 2000 "Hey Papi" video) fea-tures in her industry-rocking 2005 memoir *Confessions of a Video Vixen*. Jay Z, Ice-T, Ja Rule, Doctor Dre, Bobby Brown, P-Diddy, Xzibit, Usher, Lil' Wayne, Fred Durst, Vin Diesel, and Shaquille O'Neal are among the entertainment giants she recounts bedding and popping ecstasy with in the early 2000s when she worked as a video model and earned the moniker "Superhead." Many clutched pearls and wagged fingers at her revelations, branding her a Jezebel and suggesting she be ashamed of herself. But Karrine never has been. She's not shy about her transactional sex: "To stay afloat, I had to hustle . . . being hip hop's version of a prostitute—sleeping with men in the industry, both artists and label executives, for which I received money."[18] But she's also clear this makes her no bet-ter or worse than the men she fucked. "I'm a woman and I can suck as many dicks as I want, just as men can suck as many pussies and asses as they want. And believe me, they do! . . . You can't slut shame me, bruh," she posted. "You've got all these men out here taking dicks on Monday, snatching pussies on Tuesday, sucking anybody's ass on Wednesday, licking their bestie's nuts on Thursday, beating their wife on Friday, raping women on Saturday, praising the LORD on Sunday and you want to shame a woman for having sex?"[19]

Not satisfied with calling out men's sluttiness, Karrine reminds Black Twitter that renowned black women come with "hoe histories," too. A month before *Lemonade*'s release a Twitter war was ignited by her proud memory of being a best-selling author and *Oprah* guest at age twenty-six. Users shot back: "You sucked dick. Honestly, that ain't the route I want" and "I look up to Oprah. I want to be a woman like Oprah not you. Everything you do is tasteless." Not having any of it, Karrine volleyed, first, that she certainly *had* just sucked a dick—her husband's—underscoring continuities between "ho" and "wifey" sex; and second, that Oprah *was* like her—"Oprah was a hoe. She was promiscuous after her rape, admittedly." She expanded: "Oprah was promiscuous. Maya Angelou was a prostitute. Believing a woman worthy of praise has never had a sexual or ill reputed past is silly. So many great women have had horrible reputations. Take a long, hard look at our strong, honorable black women and see how their sex plays a part in their stories."[20] Snatching back *ho* and passing it out as a badge of honor, Karrine demands that readers honor black women for what Robin Boylorn calls "ratchet respectability." Instead of dividing black women into ratchet versus respectable, "ratchet respectability is an effort to . . . humanize black women's experiences without demonizing them": to insist that ratchet sisters deserve respect, too, that "black women can use ratchetness to resist and challenge hegemonic norms and that most black women (or at least those I know, myself included) can be both ratchet and respectable (sometimes at the same time, sometimes situationally)."[21]

Karrine writes lots of things I find unhelpful, like her woman-to-woman advice that anal sex is best saved for husbands.[22] But she also writes things that blow up tired sexual scripts in ways I adore—like her clarification that anal sex goes both ways in her marriages: "I have a strap on named Pinky. Ask my ex husbands. I will make a straight man love dick in a heartbeat and I'm not ashamed of any of it."[23] Always and everywhere, Karrine shows up to give us ratchet feminism's foundational lesson: that everyone has some ratchet in them, some part of them unapologetically partaking in what's "foolish, ignorant, ho'ishness, ghetto, and a dance" (to borrow from Stallings).[24] Oprah, Maya, Coretta Scott King, Michelle Obama, Beyoncé Knowles-Carter—it's important to imagine our black women icons have sketchy sexual histories and ghetto moments *whether they actually do or not*. Because only when we imagine ratchetness as a tool able to serve the best and brightest among us can we build solid defenses against slut shaming; only when we believe ratchetness isn't below us—and sometimes just might be above us—can we disarm the charge of *ratchet, thot, chickenhead, hoe,* and any epithet meant to keep black women in our sexual place. "A woman is all things," Karrine's *Lemonade* reflection opens. "She is your Becky. She is your Beyoncé. She is the embodiment of all that is light, all that is dark, all that is all. She is your wife. She is your whore. She is your priestess and your infidel."[25] Claiming this complexity and challenging us to do the same, Karrine can declare: "I am a woman and I cannot be broken. Especially not over some dick, chile. Now, bend over and open up."[26]

* * *

Not content to cast herself as just any old ho now that she's throwing off dutiful wifey-ness, Beyoncé shows up in "6 Inch" outfitted as a divine whore. The flowing-haired singer sits regally on the car-park cement floor, her tight-bodiced, full-length scarlet gown billowing under her and a bracket of fire surrounding her. "God was in the room when the man said to the woman, 'I love you so much. Wrap your legs around me. Pull me in, pull me in, pull me in,'" her voiceover rasps.

"Sometimes when he'd have her nipple in his mouth, she'd whisper, 'Oh, my God.' That, too, is a form of worship." God is in the car park, too: or maybe the Brazilian spirit Pomba Gira, divine harlot and mistress of red witchcraft. Beyoncé's styling evokes caramel-skinned Pomba Gira's long, wavy tresses and signature scarlet "gowns with close-fitting bodices and ample skirts," and the fire ring around her honors Pomba Gira's divine element.[27] "No one can contain fire, no one can contain her as well," a devotee explains. "Because Pomba Gira is a woman of fire, you see?"[28] When you need to make a lover come, go, stay, or return—when s/he needs to be reminded God was in the room when you were inside each other—Pomba Gira is the spirit Umbanda and Quimbanda practitioners turn to. "While her magic is capable of anything, she is particularly skilled in all matters dealing with women, the erotic, and love," ConjureMan Ali notes. "She combines her sensuality with her sorcery in the most lethal of witchcrafts; with a look she can inspire lust and love in the hearts of even the coldest of humans, or lay waste to her enemies."[29] *This, too, is a form of worship.*

Pomba Gira is the divine image of ratchetry. To entice her to work for you, you give her the most ghetto fabulous gifts: Martini & Rossi pink champagne, cherry-red lipstick, strong perfume, costume jewelry bling. A "woman of ill repute" in her lifetime, Pomba Gira's spirit hovers as an intermediary between humans and divine power. All the ratchet mess you wouldn't pray to God for—your ex's impotency, your pussy's addictiveness, your boo's sexual magic—you ask of her, because she understands why you'd need those things in a world that's often ungodly for black women seeking love. "The vulgar see her as a whore to be bought, but the wise recognize her as Woman unfettered by the restraints of society and brimming with sexual potency and sorcery. She is sex for the purpose of sex, love for the purpose of love, and best knows the human heart."[30] Pomba Gira gives black women permission to access the ratchetness inside us and use that ratchetness for a divine purpose: supporting black women's lives and loves. In *Holy Harlots: Femininity, Sexuality, and Black Magic in Brazil*, Kelly Hayes tells the story of how devotee Nazaré da Silva called on Pomba Gira to help best her husband Nilmar. When Nilmar started sleeping with the maid, Nazaré was oblivious for months—but not Pomba Gira, who woke her devotee up one night to find them *in flagrante*. Pomba Gira fired Nazaré up to throw the maid out and take her own lover to get the *good good* Nilmar hadn't been delivering. Reflecting on this tale, Hayes sees "women's stories about Pomba Gira . . . usually lead to a redefinition of roles for the couple in a way that benefits the woman," and frames Pomba Gira's intercession as a kind of ratchet feminism: "a form of gendered discourse, a set of resources and an articulatory framework through which women . . . negotiate the relations of power within which they find themselves and attempt to pursue their own interests in situations marked by inherent inequalities and conflicts."[31]

Earlier in *Lemonade*, Beyoncé paid tribute to another goddess honored in Brazil. "In 'Hold Up,' the album's second single, Beyoncé appears as Oshun, a Yoruba water goddess of female sensuality, love and fertility," Kamaria Roberts and Kenya Downs explain. "Oshun is often shown in yellow and surrounded by fresh water. Donning a flowing yellow Roberto Cavalli dress, gold jewelry and bare feet, Beyoncé channels the orisha, or goddess, by appearing in an underwater dreamlike state."[32] Practitioners of Afro-Brazilian religions cast Oshun and other orishas as "spirits of the right," who are "said to work only for good, that is, in ways that accord with dominant moral codes."[33] But Pomba Gira rolls with a rougher group of spirits: "the 'line of the left,' considered by some practitioners to be less 'evolved.' . . . As entities connected to the cut-throat world of the street, they offer decisive action unfettered by considerations of domestic virtue, loyalty, or affection."[34] Oshun and Pomba Gira are both sorceresses who bring divine creativity to love, sex, and womanness, but in different ways. Early in *Lemonade*'s journey to healing, Oshun's "elevated," dreamlike image of black womanhood uplifts the narrator in her pain; but deeper on her path she needs Pomba Gira's explosion of ratchetness to blow up the obstacles blocking her path. "Pomba Gira is a woman with seven husbands," warns a popular song, "don't mess with her, that girl is dangerous."[35] Because sometimes, Beyoncé models, you got to be that bitch.

* * *

Ride round in that, flawless. I opened the first-ever day of Beyoncé Feminism showing "Flawless," and the packed-out front row of black women and gay men not only sang but *danced* along with Queen Bey. That's when I knew these black feminist students hadn't come to play—and to do them justice, every day of teaching had to become a creative endeavor. I routinely sidelined PowerPoints to talk about black feminist issues *they* brought up, and like any live performer found myself improvising with the media I had at hand: my body and its stories. One day we were talking about respectability politics and the ways women feel we have to dress on campus to be taken seriously. Pointing to my glad lamé stilettos I told them my husband's fears about colleagues judging or predators targeting me, then admitted I wanted a "CAKE BY THE POUND" shirt but was afraid of university reactions. After students encouraged me to walk my talk about letting go of the strand of respectability politics I was hanging onto, I came in the next week wearing exactly that shirt in lavender. Another morning we were talking about identity abuse— a partner's use of gender, sexual, racial, religious, or other slurs to humiliate, intimidate, or manipulate—and I told them about a white ex-girlfriend whose physical abuse was preceded by identity-based taunts. Once (I told them) she complained I was too sexually adventurous and asked, "Did you ever think that maybe women of color just *are* more sexual than white women?" My answer: "I've slept with enough white women to know that's not true." My own mentor, the late VèVè Clark, imparted that black feminist pedagogy means *teaching for life*. And I spun these improvised lessons to model that instead of crossing our legs and denying our sexuality, black women sometimes have to be publicly creative with our bodies—so we can feel out, experiment in, and play toward an erotic freedom that doesn't exist yet. *Flossin' on it, flawless.*

* * *

In April 2016, alongside Karrine Steffans, another former stripper and video vixen was also busy trying to break the internet: newly pregnant Blac Chyna, who took to Instagram to broadcast her seven-carat diamond engagement ring from Rob Kardashian and their post-popped-the-question celebration at Los Angeles strip club Ace of Diamonds. One-time BFF to Rob's reality TV star sister Kim, Chyna was thrown to the social media wolves by the Kardashian-Jenner clan when her first baby daddy, rapper Tyga, took up with Kim and Rob's sixteen-year-old sister Kylie. So when Chyna resurfaced on the arm of the notoriously reclusive only Kardashian son—carrying the first Kardashian child of the next generation and heir to millions, no less—the internet exploded. Commenters hailed her as a *gold digger, whore, stripper, bitch*—sometimes with venom, sometimes with appreciation for her finesse in infiltrating the family that once brushed her off like dust on their Jimmy Choos. Saluting Chyna's social media triumph as "the PR equivalent of Venus rising fully formed from the foaming sea with an engagement ring in one hand and a pregnancy announcement in the other," Sylvia Obell of BuzzFeed admired: "While no one and everyone was watching, Chyna was making calculated moves to close in on her own empire with a precision and finesse that not even the Kardashians saw coming. . . . So the Kardashians, a family often accused of stealing black men, black features, and black culture, got beat at their own game by a black woman. And not just any black woman, but a video vixen who was never supposed to see the inside of the country clubs the Kardashians frequented."[36] Chyna's Venus moment splashes across social media carrying ratchet feminism's second lesson: ratchetness is all about creativity—about imagining new possibilities to navigate misogynoir with the assets we're given, including our own asses.

Gold digger, hoe, stripper, bitch, slut: these are words Blac Chyna *literally* attached to herself at the 2015 VMAs, when she and SlutWalk organizer Amber Rose wore matching skintight outfits whose fabric was painted with misogynist insults in block neon letters. "We basically wanted to paint a picture of what everybody, kind of like, already says about us," Chyna explained in a preshow interview, making clear that for her, claiming the titles *stripper* and *gold digger* is a creative decision.[37] Her sex work, whether at fabled Miami strip club King of Diamonds or the Calabasas house of a depressive millionaire, has always been art. Dance scholar Jessica Berson notes that stripping is an artistically rigorous form that shares principles with modern dance: "Striptease dance, like a number of contemporary dance techniques, emphasizes a multi-unit movement of the torso (an articulation of the hips separate from movements of the ribcage and shoulders), successive flow of motion through the joints (wave-like, 'smooth' movements of the upper body), and an implicit and explicit acknowledgment of the pelvis as the center."[38] Skillful as her dancing is, though, what set Chyna apart at KOD was her visual art—her self-aestheticizing. Radio personality Angela Lee remembers her "distinctive look—she looked like some-one who was going to be famous."[39] In an August 2016 *Elle* interview with Chyna, Lola Ogunnaike spins out: "That look would earn her thousands of dollars—'The most I've ever made in one night is $15,000,' Chyna says—and legions of fans who were enamored with her otherworldly curves, elabo-rate floral tattoos, the cheek piercings that dotted her dimples, and her long, platinum wigs with heavy bangs."[40] Whether on the VMA red carpet or the KOD stage, Chyna uses her body as a canvas: one that pops with bold colors, floral designs, silky textures, and well-placed sparkle.

Chyna put her artistic skills to work in her relationship with Rob, too. After a painful breakup with singer Rita Ora in December 2012 Rob became a near shut-in, ballooning as he gorged on junk food (spending $13,000 a month in take-out) and worrying his family as he cut them off to the point of missing Kim's wedding. But like a bawse bitch Pygmalion, Chyna rebuilt his body and confidence: "Rob A. C. (after Chyna) exercises, eats home-cooked meals, and happily en-gages with fans on social media."[41] As older sister Khloe rec-ognized begrudgingly, "Some pussy's getting him to remove his braces and shave his beard and work out."[42] So yes, Chyna showed she could be the artist of an upgraded Rob. But she also showed she could be an artist of life, one who wields the ultimate creative skill: conjuring beauty out of negativity. "She's one of those people you could just go to with any of your problems, and Chyna just makes it seem like it's a piece of cake," sister-friend Paige appreciates in the premiere of the reality show *Rob & Chyna*. "Like, 'What's wrong?' And you'd be like, 'My leg's falling off' and she's like, 'Girl! I know who could fix that.'"[43] Because that's the art of ratchet feminist life: "creatively reconstructing Black life each and every day from the ruins handed to us"[44] by a misogynoir America that calls us sluts, gold diggers, and hoes, not imagining we're alchemists who can turn shit into fashion gold. The premiere also finds Chyna, Rob, and friend Scott Disick looking through Rob's collection of Kardashian family portraits, pulling out an impressionist-style painting of the sisters in Edwardian dresses. Laughing at the expensive ratchetness of this gaudy art, Chyna claims, "I actually painted it." Then, in her pink sports bra and leggings showing off her tattoos and baby bump, she squats open-kneed in front of the painting—dwarfing the painted Kardashian sisters with her real-life curves—and smiles over her shoulder to announce: "I'ma fit right here."[45] Yes, Chyna, paint yourself into the life you dream.

* * *

When Beyoncé invokes Pomba Gira in *Lemonade*'s parking garage, she calls down a spirit known for her fierce, loving protection of all sex workers and their creative profit-making. "I know one group of strippers who set up a shrine to her backstage," Lilith Dorscy recounts, "and she granted them wealth and success for every dollar they stuffed into her spiritual g-string."[46] In "Partition," Beyoncé rode Jay Z's limo to Paris's avant-garde cabaret Crazy Horse to perform her own version of the club's legendary "Upside Down" show—a dazzling display of legs, lights, and mirrors she dances purely for pleasure. "The day I got engaged was my husband's birthday and I took him to Crazy Horse and I remember thinking, 'Damn, these girls are fly,'" she explains the fantasy behind the video. "And I just thought it was the ultimate sexy show: 'I wish I was up there, I wish I could perform that for my man . . .' so that's what I did for my video."[47] But in "6 Inch," her red-lit dance behind anonymous peep-show glass solicits money rather than love and is cosmopolitan only in the currency she collects. "She's stacking money, money everywhere she goes /You know, pesos out of Mexico," she sings the first time the camera captures her behind the glass.[48] In "Partition," Susannah Sharpless saw the main character as an *objet d'art* created by "an impressive alchemic performance with Beyoncé as a powerful magician, turning her beauty into power: over her life, over her work, and over her audience."[49] And "6 Inch" reprises this alchemy, but relocates it from a Paris of Beyoncé's fantasies to the kind of streets where Pomba Gira's protégées work their magic for "them commas and them decimals."[50]

From Nelly's "Tip Drill" (2003) to The Migos' "Freak No More" (2014), strip clubs teeming with green bills and jiggling asses are a standard video trope of Dirty South hip hop, a genre whose hits often debut in strip clubs. But bathed in ominous red instead of go-ahead green, the sex industry scene in "6 Inch" forgoes the orgiastic glitz of a corporate strip club for the lonelier, touch-me-not stage of a peep show. No doubt, Beyoncé's choice of the seedier peep show strips away hip hop fantasies of balling in the club or taking strippers home. "The peep show customer enters an individual size booth and places quarters in the motorized window to view the women dancing nude," sex worker Siren d'Lore explains the difference between strip clubs and peep shows. "It is common knowledge that these customers masturbate while enjoying the show. The peep show customer pays anywhere from twenty-five cents to a few dollars for this entertainment. The strip club is much more expensive. For the most part, masturbation is an unacceptable activity."[51] But setting the video in a peep show also links its sex work to artistic work. Long before it became associated with striptease, the peep show originated in Renaissance Europe as popular traveling entertainment and a common medium for Dutch Golden Age artists. Scenes of beautiful landscapes and epic tales were painted on the interior sides of a box, and when customers paid to look through the peephole scenes had the illusion of three-dimensionality. "What wondrous sights there were to visit: distant lands, never before seen and perhaps never before even heard of, ferocious battles and stately monuments, images to startle and delight," Richard Balzer explains the draw in *Peepshows: A Visual History*. "The mysterious box beckoned with a glimpse of a world well beyond one's self . . . the box suggested escape from the boundaries of everyday life."[52] With the stage as the box and their bodies as a medium, isn't this what peep-show dancers still do for clients?

"6 Inch" also pays homage to the unacknowledged artistry of women in Beyoncé's own medium, black popular music. Her character dances on the peep-show stage the first time she sings, "She don't have to give it up cause she's professional"—the music slowing and grinding to a halt during the last word, a series of images of violence and sex work flashing across the screen in silence until an eerie sample from Isaac Hayes's "Walk on By" sounds. This sample, which returns as a hook throughout the song, features backup singers Pat and Diane Lewis and Rose Williams hauntingly vocalizing *walk on, walk on*. "As Beyoncé loops his singers, she hints at other black women 'behind' his song: Dionne Warwick, who originally recorded 'Walk on By' in 1964, and Carla Thomas, whose hits helped establish Stax as a viable Southern soul label in the first place, though she would soon be overshadowed by her male peers," Emily Lordi insightfully points out. "By reviving these women, even as spirits or shadows, Beyoncé performs her most powerful act of black feminist alchemy. Soul music, like the blues, is filled with other women . . . *Lemonade* turns the *other women* that are its stated concern into allies."[53] Because this, *this* is why Pomba Gira and Oshun are both queen sorceresses: for the black women they protect to get their due, you need power beyond the everyday. In *Flash of the Spirit*, Robert Farris Thompson reflects how West African women's devotion to Oshun and other divine sorceresses emerges as an act of resistance to male privilege. In patrilineal Yoruba societies, where men claimed most positions of political power, women claimed the power of witchcraft to "use that power against the institutions of society" and "militate against . . . total male dominance."[54] *Walk on*, yes, *walk on.*

* * *

The day before I gave a midterm to the Beyoncé Feminism course in 2017, I received notification that two alumnae had filed charges against me for sexual harassment. Their claim: that I wore short skirts and high heels as a seduction ruse. Why they really filed this claim, I'm sure I'll never know. But their accusations hit me where I live. It felt like they were shaming me for daring to dress like a high femme, for aestheticizing my body, for dressing for pleasure and creativity rather than respectability. As graduates of Beyoncé Feminism, shouldn't they have known better than to play on the misogynoir that imagines all black women are always already making themselves sexually available? Humiliated as I was, I made a conscious decision not to change how I dressed. The next week I went to Atlanta to give a talk about *Lemonade* and outfitted myself in a white tiger faux fur coat, a low-cut jumpsuit, and six-inch sculpture platforms covered in spikes. After my presentation, a group of black undergraduates came up to me. One thanked me for the way I dressed: *you don't usually see professors do that,* she told me, *I appreciate you being brave enough to be who you are.* I don't remember that woman's name, but if you happen to read this and recognize yourself— please know at that moment I almost cried with gratitude. Because when those of us black women who choose to shake off respectability politics recognize each other, appreciate each other, see the risks we take with our bodies and applaud each other for them: this is a lifesaving gesture. The sexual harassment claim was quickly dismissed. Without the kind words of that young Atlanta sister, though, I don't know how I would have gotten through those weeks of doubting the choices I made with my body. "I'm with some flawless bitches, 'cause they more than pretty," Nicki Minaj tells everyone on the "***Flawless" remix—and never forget, us flawless booshes gotta stick together.[55]

* * *

Oh yes, booshes *gotta* stick together to make it through. "The bitch is back in ATL," Joseline Hernandez announced triumphantly on VH1's *Love and Hip Hop: Atlanta* the Monday after *Lemonade* broke the internet. Aspiring Puerto Rican reggaeton artist Joseline and her producer-lover Stevie J became the pot-stirring, mud-slinging, mess-starting couple viewers loved to hate on this black woman–centered reality show, and after a brief stint in Los Angeles the pair returned to the show that made them famous. "We're back here, don't feed into the ratchetness," Stevie counseled Joseline as she picked out a jewelry store's biggest diamond to console herself for leaving Hollywood. Joseline replied without missing a beat: "Oh, I *gotta* feed into the ratchet."[56] Like Chyna, Joseline started her career as a sixteen-year-old stripper at Miami's King of Diamonds and Diamond Cabaret, where she was arrested twice for lewd and lascivious behavior and appeared in a failed Showtime pilot about Miami strippers. She was also out as "something you call 'bisexual.' . . . When I was fourteen, I told my oldest brother that I liked women," she explained in season 4. "I'm all for the LGBT community because I'm one of them."[57] The Puerto Rican Princess (her chosen nickname) brings this lifetime of dramatic skills to her starring *Love and*

Hip Hop role: sleeping and brawling with Stevie's other women while constantly reminding them she's the Baddest Boosh of the ATL, thank you very much.

Joseline hijacked the season 5 reunion show with a surprise announcement she was pregnant by her now-estranged lover, and months of court-ordered paternity tests, drug tests, and restraining orders—accompanied by a nasty Twitter war—ensued between Stevie and his fifth baby mama. But in December 2016, the eight-months-pregnant Puerto Rican Princess took a break from this drama to "throw the biggest baby shower that anybody's seen in the world." "Everything I've been through with my baby daddy, I chose to say, you know, we ain't dealing with that. This is a celebration of life," she explains to her party planners. "We want dancers, we want people swinging from the ceiling, we want it all." One of the planners crosses herself when Joseline demands strippers at the shower, and the mother-to-be rolls her eyes at the request she consider ballerinas instead. After all, she's very public about her informed opinion strippers are some of the best women around—"I've never met a bad stripper in my life. I always meet young girls that are trying to do something with their life. I can say this for a fact"—so who better to welcome her daughter to the world? She also requests a cake with a replica of her, naked, "baby coming out the kutty cat." When the planners groan in protest, asking who'd want to eat a cake with pubic hair frosting, she rejoins: "Honey this is a *party*, this is not a funeral." Joseline gets her baby shower wishes in the end, and the guests who fly in include her Miami-based family and her Los Angeles–based lover Nikki Mudarris. Nikki treats her to a prenatal massage and, rubbing oil on her belly, promises an orgasm strong enough to bring on labor. "Miss Nikki is not only a great sexual partner of mine, she's also a good friend," Joseline waxes sentimental in her confessional.

"And I really can appreciate the fact that she came all the way from LA just to really be there for me."[58]

With her stripper-on-stripper, bad-boosh-on-bad-boosh love, Joseline's televised shower offers ratchet feminism's most important lesson: when life gets real, sisters are there for each other first, second, and third. Cooper hails ratchet feminism's birth in "the female-focused friendship that can exist between Black women (whose performances of race and class are read as lowbrow or low-class), despite the complicated and messy relationships we have with men, and oftentimes with each other," and recognizes: "This iteration, inspired by women on *Love and Hip Hop*, suggests that regardless of how ratchet or reckless we may act, sisters have each other's back when it counts."[59] Black feminism doesn't require women to be saintly with each other; jealousy, pettiness, conflict, and backstabbing are part of the human experience we shouldn't have to whitewash. But like Joseline, ratchet feminist sisters remember "we all came from a woman, got our name from a woman and our game from a woman."[60] Much as she loves her stripper sistren and fights with them, Joseline dreams of a world where black girls have safer, more lucrative possibilities for earning money. "It's just something that I feel young girls should not do," she explains about stripping. "Do not go in that strip club at all. It is a death trap. I'm going to have a foundation for young girls. We need that for young girls. We need to make this world a better place with these young girls."[61] Welcome to the world, Princess Bonnie Bella Hernandez, your mother has been dreaming of you and your freedom. "When Bonnie Bella gets here, I want to be able to show her life isn't always certain, and she could do whatever she wants to do," she explains the message behind her anti-respectable baby shower.[62] Yes, mama, yes. Because sometimes when love becomes a grind, the best thing you can do is love your fellow grinders.

✳ ✳ ✳

Pomba Gira comes once, Pomba Gira comes again. As The Weeknd begins the first verse of "6 Inch," his voice suddenly grinds to a halt and the video cuts to an image of Beyoncé in a high-necked, floor-length red-and-black brocade gown, standing in a dark room ominously swinging a red light on a chain. Shadowy and dilapidated, the room's ornate lamps, Georgian fireplace, striped chairs, and valanced drapes recall a decrepit, haunted version of "octoroon parlors"—brothels staffed by light-skinned women of color in turn-of-the-twentieth-century New Orleans. Beyoncé's red light illuminates a cadre of black women in antique clothes, furs, and jewelry—"black women that history has cast into shadows . . . a quiet army of these women who have worked too hard for the money"[63]—stationed unsmilingly on chairs and settees much as Storyville prostitutes sat in brothel parlors on display for potential customers. But this scene of beautiful black whores has turned from seduction to menace: "Every fear, every nightmare, anyone has ever had," Beyoncé's voiceover names the interlude. The brothel returns again at the close of "6 Inch," this time cutting between the octoroon parlor and a closed bedroom door engulfed in flames Beyoncé walks away from. Swinging her red light mesmerizingly in the eerie parlor, is Beyoncé's Pomba Gira casting a spell? Walking by the red light of the whorehouse fire, is she witnessing that spell come to fruition? Suddenly the song's opening lines take on a more literal, more powerful meaning: *Goddamn, she murdered everybody and I was her witness.*[64]

Remember, remember, remember. All black sex work comes out of a particular historical context, Stallings reminds us,[65] and the evocation of octoroon parlors in "6 Inch" carries a powerful historical lesson: when hoes work together, they should *never* be underestimated. The "naked dance" halls and sex shows of Storyville—New Orleans's legal red-light district that operated 1898–1917, drawing sex tourists with interracial sex, male prostitutes, BDSM, and jazz—are predecessors of contemporary strip clubs and peep shows where Karrine, Chyna, and Joseline got their start. Among the district's most powerful players were octoroon madams like Lulu White and Countess Willie Piazza, infamous "bad booshes" who made fortunes off white men's fantasies of black feminine debauchery and wielded their power to benefit prostitutes of color. Fiercely protective, Countess Piazza once shot dead the son of a high-ranking cleric who forced an employee into a nonconsensual sex act (and no one dreamed of prosecuting her). In 1917, when the city attempted to impose racial segregation in Storyville by forcing madams and prostitutes of color uptown, Piazza, White, and nearly twenty other prostitutes of color filed suit against the city. Piazza won her case in the Louisiana Supreme Court, marking one of the earliest legal victories against the South's Jim Crow laws—yet Piazza's case has all but disappeared from canonical civil rights histories. "Ideas about respectability, especially as they applied to African American and mixed-race women, help to explain why Piazza's story and the significance of her legal victory have not been adequately analyzed," Alecia Long explains.[66] Unencumbered by such respectability politics, ratchet feminist historical visions like Beyoncé's come to shine red light on the ways "women of ill repute" have *always* been a credit to the race.

Because let's be clear: ratchet women aren't dismissed, distrusted, disrespected, and disavowed simply out of prudishness. Aspiring patriarchs and their collaborators want to put ratchets "in their place" because they have the potential to be dangerous to entrenched racial, sexual, and gender inequalities. As Hayes writes of Pomba Gira, every ratchet black woman is transgressive in the way "she defies patriarchal criteria of feminine respectability. Because these criteria are predicated on channeling female sexuality in ways that maintain patriarchy and its hierarchical relations of gender, this defiance is conceptualized . . . as a dangerous sexuality that threatens the social and moral order."[67] Sex-positive feminists are unafraid to say *fuck me*, but ratchet feminists are also unafraid to say *fuck you* to patriarchy's rules—and, as Audre Lorde told us, "women so empowered are dangerous."[68] Black women, when we own our ratchetness, use it creatively, and join forces with our ratchet sistren, we're a force to be reckoned with. Yes, we'll work hard to get what we deserve. Yes, we'll learn to love the grind and make the grind love us. Yes, we'll burn the motherfucker down if we need to. *Yes yes yes yes yes*, girl, yaaasss. Don't you want to ride with us, now? People may pretend but you know, *know*, we will never be forgotten.

UNAPOLOGETICALLY FEMME

"We've been down with Texas-bred cultural sensation Beyoncé Knowles since she was a 'Bootylicious' 'Survivor' who sound-tracked our living room get-downs," the event description began. "These days she's a Super Bowl show–stealing, alleged Illuminati queen-pin who breaks the internet the way most people break bread."[1] On August 18, 2016, the *Austin-American Statesman* "put together a team of Austin's top Bey-ologists from the worlds of art, media and academia to unpack the hot sauce in 'Yoncé's bag (swag)" to host "Hold Up: The Beyoncé Feminist Sing-Along" at downtown Austin's Alamo Drafthouse.[2] I was on stage beside playwright Florinda Bryant, YouTube star Evelyn Ngugi, musician Qi Dada Ras, and music reporter Deborah Sengupta Stith, seated in front of a screen playing *Lemonade* clips to a packed house of women, femmes, and queens primed by beer and mixed drinks. After the first song, "Sorry," our moderator Deborah turned to me to open comments. And I—without even a drop of alcohol in my system, y'all—stopped everything to gush about how amazing it was to be in front of a ginormous moving image of Queen Bey in a Zana Bayne bullet bra, so close I could almost reach out and stroke her royal boob. Everyone laughed at my silly display of femme-on-femme desire, then joyfully went on to tout the video's highlights: the "Boy Bye" bus, African body paint and prints, Becky with the good hair, and of course, record-smashing tennis star Serena Williams twerking for Beyoncé.

Not just a Beyoncé sing-along, mind you; this was a Beyoncé *feminism* sing-along, with all proceeds benefiting a local women's shelter. Back when Beyoncé stood in front of a brightly lit screen declaring herself "FEMINIST" at the 2014 VMAs, not everyone was here for it. Eurythmics singer Annie Lennox publicly shot down her feminist credentials by branding the artist's stance *feminism lite*, decrying her example as noxious to young women fascinated by the "overtly sexual thrust" of her performances, and summing up her disapproval with the quip: "twerking is not feminism."[3] On this hot, rainy August night two years later, though, not only was a sold-out, drunk-singing Alamo Drafthouse celebrating Serena twerking for Beyoncé as feminism: when I publicly longed for Beyoncé's boob and Serena's thighs, our viewing of "Sorry" also became a platform—platform as in the stage, platform as in my heels—to celebrate black femme-inism and black femme desire. Featuring a parade of dancing, decorated black women who have nothing to say to men but *bye*, "Sorry" opens space for viewers like me to see Beyoncé's "sexual thrust" aimed at other black women and femmes. Why, after all, would Lennox assume women choose "glamour, femininity, and femme presentations" for men's pleasure *only*, as Janet Mock pointedly questions? "Our 'dressed-up' bodies and 'big hair'" don't mean we're "colluding with patriarchy, using only our bodies rather than our brains," Mock reminds us in defense of Beyoncé's sexiness.[4] *Hell nah*, as Bey sings.

Remember the "Flawless" remix, when Beyoncé and Nicki Minaj stroke each other on stage in Paris as Nicki raps: "Uhn! This every hood nigga dream, fantasizing about Nicki and B"?[5] Or the "Yoncé" video, where Victoria's Secret model Joan Smalls licks Yoncé's cleavage while she stands on a Brooklyn street and stares naughtily at the camera? Yes, Beyoncé's been daring us to look at her and see femme-on-femme desire for a while now. But in *Lemonade*, Beyoncé Knowles (of the Iberia Parish, Louisiana, Beyincés) brings black femme love *home*, to the River Road plantations and New Orleans streets that represent her ancestors' homespace. She gives us what femme scholar Gayatri Gopinath calls a *queer region*: an imaginary somewhere black femmes can act out their love *Southernly*, in a Storyville brothel, on the front porch, or at a women's revival meeting.[6] In "Hood Femmes and Ratchet Feminism," Ashleigh Shackelford calls out the narrowness of how we imagine black femme-ness by asking: "What about the bisexual trap queens, the queer hood femmes, or the sexually fluid thotties?"[7] And, *Lemonade* left me wondering, what about down-home-bred, hot-sauce-carrying, Mardi Gras–celebrating, Texas Bama femmes? Where can we get some love for ourselves, and where do we find space to love each other as hugely as Beyoncé moves with Serena on screen?

These next pages are a snapshot of my journey in search of the kind of Southern black femme space I see sprawled out so grandly in "Sorry." I can't tell you everything I've witnessed, but I do want to show you a little of the femme love I've found in different Southern cities I've passed through—Austin and Atlanta and New Orleans—and I want to show you how I see black femmes making space for our lives and loves wherever we are, carving out room in the cracks and fissures of the white, straight worlds always threatening to hem us in. Will my route be easy to follow? Probably not—I'm not known for being easy any more. I'll be curlicuing my own queer kind of femme map that moves in no straight lines and circles around on itself, sashays between real places I've been and fantasy places I've seen in Beyoncé videos, and stops to appreciate sparkles and nice asses where I find them. Come along on my own version of the "Boy Bye," ladies and femmes, and please enjoy the ride.

FIRST STOP: ATLANTA

Originally from California, Che Johnson-Long is a queer black femme, community organizer, and herbalist living in the city

Ebony crowned the "Black Mecca of the South"—Atlanta. The Big Peach is also the birthplace of the Femme Mafia, founded in 2005. Lesbian magazine *Curve* tells the story of its formation this way: one night when "Aly Stealey and some fellow femmes donned sparkly makeup, short skirts, and fierce heels to Atlanta's lesbian hot spit My Sisters' Room," bartenders refused to serve them.[8] The butches they came to cruise met them with silence, and one—taking Stealey for a straight interloper—threw a lit cigarette and burned her Saturday-night dress. "Fast-forward months later, to when Stealey and her girls were welcomed with open arms at My Sisters' Room and other bars around the city . . . march in the gay and black pride parades . . . invade leather bars where, Rachael Smith says, 'the boys love us.'"[9] What happened? Aly, Rachael, and friends banded together over dinner one night to form the Femme Mafia, a celebratory, take-no-shit organization to empower femmes of all genders, races, ages, and sexualities in the queer community. "Atlanta is a very queer place, but I noticed there didn't seem to be a femme presence at all," Rachael, the Mafia's first donna, explained.[10] So the Mafia hosted internal events, where femmes came together over dinner, drinks, or dancing to support each other; and attended larger queer events, where dozens of femmes showed up together to announce their presence as a force to be reckoned with in a femmephobic culture. The group quickly grew to over a hundred members and expanded to include offshoots across the country.

I've been lucky enough to live in two cities with Femme Mafias, Minneapolis and Austin. I came out not only as lesbian but as femme in 1995—while wearing patent leather wedges and lipstick, mind—so imagine how excited I was when a Femme Mafia came to my town! The Minneapolis Femme Mafia met in apartments and coffee shops and clubs, had parties, potlucks, T-shirt contests, even bake sales to bring the Femme Porn Tour to town. I came to the first meeting with my Chicana femme friend Cindy. Now, not only were we the only femmes of color to walk through the door, we were the ones with the most makeup, highest heels, and newest clothes. We were met by a bevy of femmes in muted pants and skirts and sweater sets who enjoyed building their femme-ininities around vintage fashions of the 1940s and '50s—the last era, some imagined, when it was possible to be unapologetically fem(me)inine. "I love wearing 50s styles, looking like a proper 50s woman—but being far from it," one "vintage femme" told femme scholar Ulrike Dahl. "I know not everything was rosy back then (genocide, prejudice and so on), but there were some lovely attitudes that I wish current society would look at."[11] No, not everything was rosy back then and not everyone was, either. Cindy and I were well-tolerated outliers who not only lacked pink-and-cream skin and Scandinavian last names, but insistently chose twenty-first-century (sometimes tongue-in-cheek) fashions. Even that didn't always work, though. One Halloween I dressed in a cheerleader outfit I'd bought at my grandfather's alma mater, Miles College. I ran into a femme mafiosa that night who greeted me laughing and asking, "That's not a real school, right?"

Yes, femmes of color *are* real, and we need our own models of femme-ininity to reflect that back to us. So in 2013 Che, a lifelong organizer with a passion for Beyoncé—"you know that you're a beylieter when your phone autocorrects 'know' to 'knowles,'" one of her Facebook posts reads[12]—began hosting workshops geared toward black femme-identified folks, which she called "Yoncé Taught Me: Black Femme Formations." Black femme, she clarifies, is a femme-inine-of-center "Gender Presentation and can be expressed by your clothes, swag, energy, accessories, shoe game, spirit, hair, etc."[13] In its opening sentences, the event description makes clear the antiracist and feminist stakes of workshopping a specifically *black* femme-ininity. "In the time of Beyonce, much of what we learn about Black Femininity comes from outside of the black femm[inine] community," it begins. "How can we use our collective super powers to re-construct a flawless feminism that centers black culture?"[14] The workshop traveled to Dallas, Brooklyn, Philadelphia, Detroit, Denver, and Amherst, and Che designed a follow-up national survey—"Yoncé Taught Me: Femme of Color Needs Survey"—to build tools for future black femme organization and love.

In November 2016 a former Beyoncé Feminism student sent me a link to the survey, complete with a GIF of Beyoncé blowing kisses with impossibly red lips. And I thought, of course! Who else but Beyoncé would you build a black femme workshop around? Not only because she's (arguably) the most recognized black woman entertainer we have, someone even the Becky I almost slapped at the Halloween party knows is real. Not only because black femmes *love* her and constantly pay homage to her style, rocking "Flawless" jewelry like no one else. Most importantly, because Beyoncé's ultrafemme image tramples on the *specifically black* forms of femmephobia I grew up with. For those of us who came up hearing fem(me)ininity isn't something black women should play up if we want to be taken seriously—for those of us who were told we should be "natural" African queens without lipstick and eyelashes and sparkles and hairspray—Beyoncé reflects back that the girliest of black girls *can* run the world. Queen Bey's embrace of the self-consciously artificial—bling, makeup, extensions, and Coachella—gifts us with a model of black femininity pliable enough to valorize black cis- and transfemmes in a way Erykah Badu–style ideals of "naturalness" never could. Beyoncé loves and embraces black femmes' kind of joyfully unnatural, spectacularly artistic gender presentation, and looking at her I feel I *never* need to apologize for being black, femme, and fabulous as I want to be.

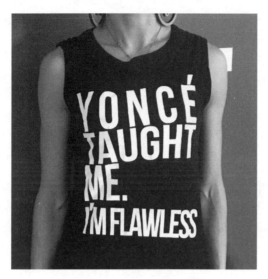

Yoncé Taught Me.
Photo by Michaela Machicote.

NEXT STOP: NEW ORLEANS

In "Sorry," Beyoncé offers us a vision of a world where black femmes are the *only* people who count. Opening on a close-up of light glancing off metal, "Sorry" begins with Beyoncé's voiceover: "What will you say about me now that you've killed me?"[15] A sad-sounding jewelry box plays as the camera pans to the interior of a moving bus, where black women in power shoes, artistic braids, and white-painted Afromysterics designs by Nigerian artist Laolu[16] sway left and right, bend at the waist and circle forward, alternate body rolls. Finally the camera finds Beyoncé and we hear: "My heaven will be a love without betrayal." The "Boy Bye" bus (as its destination sign reads) appears as the vehicle ferrying a now-killed Beyoncé to heaven *and* as the heaven she imagines: an afterlife in the love of black women, who circle, move with, and protect her in ways (lyrics accuse) her side-chick-collecting man hasn't.

These body-painted, artistically coiffed dancers could easily fit Sublimefemme's description of *high femme*: a feminine-
of-center queer gender that "uses exaggeration, artifice, and/
or theatricality to denaturalize femininity."[17] But I'd call the
distinctly Southern, unapologetically black, open-leggedly
sexual femme-ininity on the "Boy Bye" *ratchet femme*.[18] The
most African elements of black women's self-styling—
Senegalese box braids, say, or large hoop earrings like the
ones I'm wearing now—are often the first to be called ratchet.
And the fierce femme-ininity in "Sorry" is *so black* its African
roots show: in the Ankara-print jumpsuit Beyoncé wears when
she spreads her legs and invites dancers to suck on her balls,
the Masai necklaces she layers as she dances in front of the
"Boy Bye," and—most dramatically—the Afromysterics body
art that decorates Bey and her dancers. Resembling chalk
drawings, Laolu's white body paint looks *cool*: as in the Black
Atlantic *aesthetic of cool* Robert Farris Thompson sees traveling between West Africa, the US South, and the Caribbean,
"often linked to the sacred usage of water and chalk (and
other substances drenched with associations of coolness and
cleanliness) as powers which purify men and women by return
to freshness, to immaculate concentration of mind, to the artistic shaping of matter and societal happening."[19] Like deep-
colored skin, coolness—remaining unruffled, collected, on
fleek in the face of sleepless nights, side chicks, and husbandly
disrespect—is an Afrocentric aesthetic "Boy Bye" dancers
share with their Nigerian sisters.

The "Boy Bye" drives these fierce femmes somewhere
"there are no clear demarcations between reality and sur-
reality or past and present," as Chris Kelly puts it.[20] While
cars and buildings outside look like twenty-first-century New
Orleans, the "Boy Bye" has the movable windows, manual
destination sign, metal poles, riveted ceiling, and exterior
lines of mid-twentieth-century buses—the kind thousands of

black Southern women rode daily in the era of civil rights bus boycotts. Working-class black women spearheaded boycotts in Baton Rouge (1953) and Montgomery (1955), and the deuce-flashing dancers on the "Boy Bye" perform a fantasy of boycotted buses reclaimed by the women for whom they were once sites of "private misery" and public protest.[21] But where bus boycotters went out of their way to broadcast respectability—heeding movement leaders' call to "publicly exhibit many of the accepted ideals of respectable female behavior—even in the midst of their bold insurgency . . . to appear more 'lady-like' than many of their white segregationist opponents"—the "Boy Bye" riders ratchet things up on the bus and queer them, too. Like Cindy and I at the Femme Mafia, these femmes forgo the sharply pleated dresses, starched white shirts, and neatly waved hair of boycotters for platform combat boots and bodysuits. Playful eroticism circulates like hips in *this* bus as Beyoncé lifts her open legs wide to laugh and sing, "Suck on my balls, pause," and women clap for sister riders as they dance on the center pole, arch off window frames, and roll shoulders to lean in toward one another.

And when they get off the bus, things get even queerer. Starting with the second chorus and verse, "Sorry" cuts to the "Boy Bye" parked on a dark rural road—having traveled "from civilization to an open field," Kamaria Roberts and Kenya Downs believe[22]—with Bey and riders dancing in front of the bus in wide-open public space. From the waist up they publicize anger by raising middle fingers, waving palms in talk-to-the-hand circles, and "chucking my deuces": a Houston expression for waving peace fingers as a sign of dismissal—*peace out, boy.*[23] From the waist down powerful leg movements broadcast don't-care sexuality as dancers bounce low to the ground and circle hips while Queen Bey opens and closes her thighs on the hood. In front of the bus she sings: "Now you gotta see me wilding . . . And I don't feel bad about it." A note on *Lyrics Genius* wonders: "While she's wilding, is she out with her girlfriends or getting frisky on the dance floor with some other dude?"[24] But all the sexiness on the "Boy Bye" suggests she might be out with her girlfriends getting frisky with *them*. "Headed to the club . . . me and my ladies sip my D'ussé cup": yes, these unapologetically black, unapologetically (t)hot dancers plan to sip Beyoncé's liquor (you know what that's a metaphor for!) to power the "Boy Bye" to heaven.

This is one way black Southern femme-ininity makes room for itself: it weaponizes, Africanizes, sexualizes the "proper" black womanliness inherited from our badass grandmothers, like a pair of heirloom earrings we lovingly turn into nipple rings. It conjures possibilities for us not only to get on the bus where we want but to get off where we want, too. These ladies are black and sexy as they want to be, dressed and decorated to the hilt as they busride to a heaven of "love without betrayal" by ride-or-die heterocentricity, white-acting self-effacement, or siddity respectability politics.[25] And Beyoncé declares: "I ain't sorry."

NEW ORLEANS, AGAIN

A "black queer sneaker femme, parent, vegan baker, academic, performer and youth worker" living in New Orleans, Savannah Shange is the daughter of writer Ntozake Shange and mother of Harriet, a beautiful, soulful-eyed child named after the Moses of the Underground Railroad.[26] When she was voluptuously pregnant in 2014, Savannah posed with her triumphant belly for Melisa Cardona's New Orleans queer portrait series *Reflections*. According to Sonny Oram, this series "is a chapter of her larger collection of images called 'Soul Reflections,' a series of outdoor portraits that looks at the water of South Louisiana, looking at the people, looking at the water."[27] In her portrait, Savannah squats regally in front of a brightly graffitied wall reflected in the muddy, littered puddle at her feet. She wears a mudcloth-style dress, fabulously patterned Steve Madden wedges, chest-length Ankara earrings, a crown of braids, and maroon lipstick.[28] Caught in a side shot, Savannah gazes off at the horizon to the camera's right as if looking into a future (or past?) far from the flooded destruction at her feet, inviting us to look at the New Orleans *she* sees.

I adore that Cardona chose all black and brown representatives for her queer New Orleans, and especially appreciate her visibly pregnant representative. Because if there's anyone who's *never* been a poster child for mainstream LGBT movements, it's pregnant femmes of color. Since my second trimester of pregnancy I've been presumed straight, and even queer friends wondered if I'd taken up with cis men. Some asked me straight out (pun intended): *Wait, you're having a baby? Are you still dating women?* Most queer friends of my youth, though, especially those who only still see me through social media, seem to *want* to ask but are too polite. They make comments like: *Wow, how much has changed in your life! What's it like being a mom? Being married? Being . . . in Texas?* My impulse is to respond as quickly as I can type—I got pregnant through donor sperm, married a transman, and am still a professional queer! Because I fearfully project these old friends judging me as that stereotype of the femme traitor: the lesbian who's only queer when it's convenient and then, sooner or later, leaves behind the "lifestyle" to pass seamlessly into the privileges of the straight world.

But if pregnancy and motherhood put a black femme's queer credibility in jeopardy, they deepen her ties to blackness in a way nothing else can. Like me, Savannah hunted far and wide for an anonymous African American donor—and by choosing one made her daughter *black on purpose*, as she puts it. During their donor search, Savannah and her partner wrote an email to friends that declared: "Both of us have been very deeply shaped by the experience of being Black. We come from a generations-long tradition of struggle, resilience, and cultural genius against the harshest odds, one that is shared by all Black folks who are descended from enslaved Africans. We hope to pass on the power and promise of that heritage to our children, and thus we seek a Black donor."[29] Let me tell you from experience, nothing cements a black femme's commitment to radical black feminism—to the world-changing importance of black women loving each other—more than parenting a fiery, irreverent, imaginative, bear-hugging, laughing black girl who keeps you accountable to this world and its future. But blackening through motherhood comes with other implications, too. Suddenly, as an unmarried mama who ran around town with baby on hip and no baby daddy in sight, I slipped into folks' stereotypes of the irresponsible black breeder. I met sighs, impatience, and cut eyes when I carried her to my doctor's visits, meetings, and appointments at government offices. And black men took her existence as proof in the flesh I was sexually available to them. I remember men fighting to help lift her stroller on the bus then offering me company afterward. And I'll never forget three young black men calling out as I walked down the street with baby Baía, inviting me to spend time with them. When I declined one shouted: "I *know* you like black men, I see that baby!"

But finding yourself inside those old sexual stereotypes also offers chances to play with queerness and blackness in new ways. An instructor at Tulane who taught Blackness, Sexuality, and Youth the spring *Lemonade* came out, Savannah posted to her website shots of a whiteboard class discussion on "what does 'femme' do that 'feminine' does not?" One of many answers written into a beautiful blue and green circle was, "take cussing, sluttiness & taboo aspects of society as tools to ride for their community."[30] In other words, instead of trying to sidestep all those myths of sexual excess and irresponsibility, *femme* creates opportunities to tear those stereotypes of the femme fatale, welfare mama, or breeding wench up from the inside out. Think our sexiness isn't to be trusted? You shouldn't trust us, we don't want to mess with your biphobic ass anyway. Think we have babies we don't have money to raise? Maybe, but we had thousands of dollars to pay for donor sperm to make them. Think we don't know how to use birth control? The folks fucking us have pussies so we don't have to. Now stop interrupting our grinding: we have cities to represent and children to raise and femmes to ride for, just like Beyoncé and Serena.

ON TO NAPOLEONVILLE

As the opening music box slows and the "Boy Bye" riders start talking among themselves, "Sorry" cuts to its second location: the moss-draped, lemon-flowered, white-columned Greek Revival mansion at Madewood Plantation. This mansion is a real place, a former sugarcane plantation and national historic landmark near Napoleonville, Louisiana; director Khalil Joseph transforms it into a fantasy space, an opulent estate dedicated to black women's pleasure and power rather than forced labor. The opening chorus comes in as Serena Williams glides down a flying staircase sporting a black bodysuit, stiletto ankle boots, powerful bare legs, and switching hips, her long-nailed left hand trailing the banister. The camera follows her as she walks backward through the hall, turns with hair swinging, then finally stops in front of Queen Bey sitting spread-thighed in a high-backed chair, one leg slung cockily over the chair's ornate arm. Beyoncé's pose takes us back to "Déjà Vu" (2006), shot at Louisiana's Oak Alley Plantation and featuring Jay Z sprawled in the great house in a similar high-backed chair, his left leg flung over the chair's arm as Beyoncé literally bends over backward dancing for him.[31] But in "Sorry" Bey sits still as Serena twerks for *her*, fulfilling the artist's request that the generous-thighed tennis legend "just be really free and just dance like nobody's looking and go all out."[32]

Posed like Jay Z but wearing a bodysuit and stilettos like Serena, Beyoncé shows up at Madewood looking like an aggressive femme. Discussing Bey's aggressive femme style in earlier videos, Anne Mitchell explains: "The aggressive femme identity is multiplicitous, but can be characterized as a gender identity or presentation that takes charge, tops, actively initiates and participates in sexual intercourse. She takes no shit, appreciates the female body, and wants to please it."[33] Or as one black aggressive femme brags, these are "femmes who 'got they own'": own house, own throne, own dancers, own strap-on, own *whatever they need*.[34] "Aggressive"—which signifies female masculinity as a noun, but female (sexual) dominance as an adjective—came to queer lexicons from New York's ballroom scene, reaching national audiences in Daniel Peddle's documentary about black aggressive subculture.[35] Far away from that East Coast life as she sits spread-legged in a plantation foyer and watches Serena grind on the banister, Beyoncé keeps aggressive femme's blackness but gives it a Southern twist. "Sorry" moves queer femme-ininity out of the ballroom scene into the quadroon ball, away from voguing toward twerking.

With her café-au-lait skin and Creole heritage, Beyoncé could easily play the role of a beautiful, tragic quadroon bartered at a ball. Quadroon balls—where white men paid entrance fees to dance and negotiate sexual relationships with women of color—loom large in New Orleans lore, despite historians' claims that they were rare. "There is a common myth told about nineteenth century New Orleans," Laine Kaplan-Levenson reflects. "It goes something like this: Imagine you're in an elegant dance hall in New Orleans in the early 1800s. Looking around, you see a large group of white men and free women of color, who were at the time called quadroons . . . Mothers play matchmakers, and introduce their daughters to these white men, who then ask their hand in a dance. The ballroom is fancy, and the invited guests look the part."³⁶ Scenes of quadroon balls in films like *The Courage to Love* (2000) and *The Feast of All Saints* (2001) romanticize these dances into the twenty-first century, lending clichés to the Madewood shots of "Sorry": Greek Revival columns, chandeliers, candelabra, flying staircase, and black women dancers—yes, the "Boy Bye" dancers—seated in chairs against the wall.³⁷ Only color-struck male suitors are missing from Bey and Serena's ball: this party is femme-on-femme only. Now, despite their mythic part in Old South interracial romances, quadroon balls always fostered women-only eroticism. A nineteenth-century writer scoffed they were "mere places of rendezvous for all the gay females in town,"³⁸ and recent representations like *The Feast of All Saints* imagine ballrooms as glorified brothels where quadroons lived together upstairs. Nineteenth-century prostitutes who roomed together, Graham Robb finds, partnered in "brothel marriages,"³⁹ and Leonard Le'Doux's historical romance *The Belles of Chateau Vidal* imagines "quadroon marriages" between women of color who spent time between balls in lip-biting, pussy-fingering sex.⁴⁰ So why shouldn't Bey and Serena cut men out of the quadroon fantasy, since there's always been enough femme sexy to go around without them?

But Beyoncé's aggressive femme twists the quadroon fantasy harder. White male voyeurs eroticized the pleasures of dominating a helpless, passive quadroon lover—"a petted, fawning thing, of love and sin," Rixford Lincoln imagined her in "The Quadroon Ballroom" (1911).⁴¹ But instead of fawning as a petted, passive object of desire, quadroon-light Beyoncé sits tall as the femme top Serena dances for: showing she "appreciates [Serena's] body, and wants to please it"⁴² by pointing admiringly to the body-rolling athlete as she commands everyone to "stop interrupting my grinding," then raises her arms and dances in her chair as Serena twerks. Serena—whose father is from Louisiana—spectacularly refuses to perform the passive quadroon, either. Media responses to dark-skinned, powerfully muscled, Afrocentrically coiffed Serena recycle the gendered colorism that fetishized quadroons while darker women were excluded from balls. Most notorious is Russian tennis official Shamil Tarpischev's 2014 reference to Serena and sister Venus as "the Williams brothers," a comment Serena called out as "insensitive and extremely sexist as well as racist at the same time."[43] Resonating with the song's message—"I am not sorry about anything. I really connected with those lyrics and felt good about that"[44]—Serena rules as belle of the ball, and Bey's light-skinned aggressive femme celebrates the athlete's beauty without reducing her power. When they invited her for this cameo, Beyoncé's team told Serena "Sorry" was "about strength and it's about courage and that's what we see you as"[45]—and that's what she looks like, too. The young-est Williams even gets a shot posing by herself in the power chair, visualizing Bey and Serena's black femme play as power exchange rather than one-way dominance.

Outside this fantasy Madewood, the quadroon circulates as Louisiana's version of the Jezebel stereotype. "The Jezebel was portrayed as a fair-skinned, African American woman with a shapely body who was seductive, alluring, oversexed and manipulative," Danice Brown explains. "She was described as using her sexual attraction and promiscuity to receive atten-tion and material goods" and "painted as a woman focused on pleasing men, especially slave masters."[46] But these misogynoir stock images, too, can become somewhere black Southern femme-ininity makes room for itself: by dancing into the old sexual stereotypes our grandmothers were trying to avoid by respectability, and rechoreographing them so all that sexuality comes back to serve *us* instead of "pleasing men." Dance on, Bey and Serena, do Louisiana out and proud!

BACK TO AUSTIN

Block letters spell out *TWERK* on top, cursive twirls *shop* below, and in the middle a drawing of a round-cheeked booty invites everyone to "TWERK THE INAUGURATION!!: A Woman of Color Twerkshop with Shakia Williams." Shakia's blue-haloed photo stares at viewers as she perches on a chair rocking a see-through teddy, black top hat, and tattooed right thigh. "Straight out of New Orleans Bounce with roots in West African ritual dance, twerking celebrates black fem(me)inine folks' bodies, spirits, and power," the flyer declares. "Join Shakia Williams of Her Sins Burlesque & Cabaret to shake what your mama gave you and twerk for black and brown, cis and trans* women's empowerment! We invite you to connect with your body and your community as we move together like nasty women; claim our bodies as our own, ungrabbable assets; and share strategies for self-care and community-building." Born in New Jersey and living in Austin, Shakia is a pole dancer, neoburlesque artist, and former Twerk Fit instructor at Brass Ovaries aerial arts studio. When I floated the idea of an inauguration TwerkOut to my amazing colleague Jackie Salcedo she suggested I recruit Kia, a black femme goddess who, she admired, can get *anyone* to twerk. The TwerkOut filled to capacity with students who agreed. One appreciated, "I really liked how personalized it was. She took time to come to each of us and base her teaching on whatever level we were on. We all had differing degrees of experience, but we left learning something new." My black femme friend J, who *says* she didn't know how to twerk before but I don't really believe her, texted after: "I loved the opportunity to be with other women of color, in a safe space, physically moving our bodies and doing something fun, exchanging laughs, tips, insecurities, and the pleasure of moving our bodies in a way that feels good." The text ended with a flurry of bright-colored balloons.

Yes, Kia can show a femme how to move her body in lots of ways that feel good. She confessed her twerk skills were nothing compared to her pole dancing, and a few weeks later I saw the truth of that when she and fellow artists Zoja Ullesco and Shelbi Aiona went to Austin's Graffiti Park for an afternoon of outdoor pole dance. That day at the park—an unfinished three-story concrete building foundation painted and repainted by visitors—the dancers set up a pole in front of a green, blue, pink, purple and orange-swirled wall of large letters declaring "Fuck Trump" and "GOD SAVE THE QUEEN."[47] Kia joined Zoja and Shelbi spinning one on top of the other with thighs scissored together in sexy duets and trios, and soloed twirling upside down, hanging by one leg, walking on air in her platform stilettos and pink patterned bikini.[48] These high femme dancers not only brought the women's space of the dancing pole out into the open, to a graffiti culture coded as men's; they openly queered that space, dancing for each other and their friends with no men in sight. Graciela Trajtenberg considers that to make their way in an art dominated by masculinity, women graffiti artists "develop an alternative femininity: *elastic femininity* . . . that contains feminist claims together with traditional feminine characteristics" and "is fluid, multi-faceted and relational."[49] And in this graffiti park Kia performs black femme-ininity as elastic as her Lycra bathing suit, one that's as "springy, bouncy, vivacious" (to use one definition of elastic) as her twerk and "spontaneously expansive" (to use another) as her legs on a pole.

At the TwerkOut Kia let us know she wasn't teaching public classes at the moment—*but* she has a portable pole in her apartment where she gives private twerk and pole lessons.

J and I immediately decided our birthday gift to ourselves needed to be private lessons with Kia, what else? To tell the truth, I liked the idea of doing lessons in her home space—it seems like the really, really black femme way to do things. Writing about queer regions, Gayatri Gopinath reminds us we have to stop searching for queer space in bars, pride parades, and other public spaces if we want to find femmes of color. These "'other' sexual cultures may not be readily intelligible as either 'public' or 'gay': they may well be enacted by female subjects and take place not in the bar or the club but rather the confines of the home, the beauty parlor, the women's hostel," she elegantly remarks.[50] You want to find black femme space in Austin? Don't bother going downtown. Try the brunch at Priscilla and Rose's house, or the femme party at Camille's place, or the private twerk class in Kia's apartment. But remember, these spaces are invitation *only*—to keep them ours, with no one interrupting our grinding.

NAPOLEONVILLE, AGAIN

Please don't think I planned to leave Madewood without giving some appreciation to the dance Serena so expertly works for her aggressive femme: pussy-popping, booty-dropping twerking. Of course you know the dance. For better or worse, pop star Miley Cyrus mainstreamed twerking when she attempted it in a nude-colored bikini surrounded by teddy bears and black dancers at the 2013 Video Music Awards. But as a word and a dance, *twerk* comes out of Louisiana's 1990s black music scene. Twerking, Kyra Gaunt explains, is "a kind of kinetic orality that began as a black social dance in New Orleans over twenty years ago that involves bouncing your booty to the rhythmic changes and lyrical bars of a popular rap or twerk song."[51] What differentiates twerking from other African-derived booty dances like the percolator, the stripper dance, or the puppy tail, she clarifies, "is in part due of the fact that this rap-based style of song and dance emanates out of the Dirty South as opposed to the dominant realms of East and West coast commercial rap and hip hop."[52] In fact, black New Orleans *women* introduced twerking to the South. The first song with *twerk* in the title was Angela "Cheeky Blakk" Woods's 1994 "Twerk Something," and bounce choreographer Marisa Joseph claims: "You think about twerking, it came from Cheeky. No one really gives her credit."[53] Dillard University professor Terri Coleman builds on this to remind us: "Just like Cheeky doesn't get credit, New Orleans black women have never profited from the things we do—the dancing, the cooking, the making babies."[54]

No one denies twerking's debt to New Orleans's queer artists, some of its most famous ambassadors remaining hard-hitting transfeminine artists like Katey Red and Big Freedia.[55] Freedia in particular—whose reality show *Big Freedia, Queen Diva* shows her giving a Twerkshop for Tulane students, getting banned from a Mississippi stage for excessive twerking, and launching a Twerk exercise app—has been hailed as the crossover performer who "twerked [her] way into viewers' hearts" and "established [herself] as the mainstream queen of bounce." (And yes, Freedia will return in the final chapter of this book—you haven't heard the last of her.) While it's hard to ignore this transfeminine star power, recognition of twerking's queerness almost never extends to its black *lesbian* erotics. But black dykes enjoy twerking for themselves, their butches, and their femmes, too. Kimari Carter, the self-styled "feminist twerk scholar" who brought her brilliance to my first Beyoncé Feminism class and is currently working on a documentary on black women, twerking, and strip clubs, shared with me footage of two black queer dancers at Houston's Black Diamonds Club. Shot in the dressing room, the clip shows two high femmes talking excitedly over one another about how much they appreciate the "gay bitches" who come to the club. "Gay bitches know gay bitches," a self-proclaimed lesbian tells Kimari, and both rattle off stories of generous-with-tips lesbians who come to have black women twerk for them and, if they can manage it, go home with them. One declares she's always ready to fuck a "badass bitch," then looks flirtatiously at her fellow femme dancer—who laughs and asks "Why you looking at me?"[56]

Like this clip, "Sorry" opens space to revel in the sex-positive, thigh-loving, booty-celebrating black femme-inism of one high femme twerking for another—in the woman-centered eroticism of the world's most famous black women celebrating their unapologetically black, undeniably skilled asses with no one interrupting their grinding. As Serena twerks by her chair, Beyoncé tells the song's male addressee: "I ain't thinking 'bout you." And why would she? Serena drops it low to twerk with wide-open knees, twerks on the floor with one leg lifted, and body rolls low to the ground—always in front of Bey's chair but never with her ass facing the camera, keeping Queen Bey the only one in a position to enjoy it. One fantasy about twerking is that it brings dancers to orgasm,[57] and one way (I like) to read the multiple shots and multiple positions of Serena's twerking is as Beyoncé encouraging, demanding, and manipulating multiple orgasms for her dancer. "Let's have a toast to the good life," she sings after Serena rolls on the floor in front of her throne. Oh yes, Serena and Beyoncé enjoying this twerking (un)quadroon ball together looks like a sweet taste of that *good good* life.

And their *good good* life imagines my favorite way to open room for black Southern femme-ininity: carving it out in women-only spaces that have always been ours. That might be the dressing room of a strip club, yes, or a hair shop or a Sunday kitchen or an AKA sorority house. Femmes, it might even come out of our favorite girlhood spaces. Responding to mainstream media's inability to appreciate Serena's ample ass, Janell Hobson reminds us that black women shake our booties on tennis courts, dance floors, or anywhere else first and foremost to please *ourselves*. Remember, she chides, black girls learn to *shake what our mama gave us* not for boys but for *other black girls*: in "female-centered space for affirmation and pleasure in their bodies" offered by childhood games like "Little Sally Walker," "Brown Girl in the Ring," or "Lemonade."[58] My daughter taught me this last hand-clapping song, which ends with girls dancing to the chant "Turn around, touch the ground / Kick your boyfriend out of town"—in other words *boy, bye*.[59] Male hip hop artists representing the Dirty South often riff off girls' hand-clapping games, from Nelly's "Country Grammar" to Juicy J's "Miss Mary Mack." But Beyoncé is one of the few contemporary female artists to re-script these traditional black Southern texts into something for grown-ass black *women's* empowerment, and we shouldn't underestimate the importance of that. Hobson concludes: "We may need to recreate that circle of women—first enacted in childhood—who reaffirm that our bodies are fine, normal, capable, and beautiful. . . . Only then will we be able to follow the lead of Serena Williams, proudly displaying our behinds while continuing our winning streak."[60]

AUSTIN, LAST TIME

While I was writing this, a new family moved onto our block on the northernmost edge of Austin. Their oldest daughter is an outgoing, curl-haloed, sunny-dispositioned black girl who immediately decided she and Baía were going to be best friends. Soon they were having fun in the streets and running back and forth between each other's houses, playing baby and Barbie and riding scooters and bikes, trading clothes and doing each other's makeup. When Baía got to make a guest appearance in my Beyoncé Feminism class to demonstrate her skill at "Lemonade Crunchy Ice," she asked if her bestie could come demonstrate with her too—and her bestie earnestly said she could come, yes, she was so sure her mother wouldn't mind if she missed school I didn't need to bother asking. (Nice try.) She's famous for blocks around as the twerking five-year-old, and as much as she and Baía like to twerk in the house I'm sure they're doing it up and down our nice suburban street, too. Well, why not? They're Southern black girls and they're entitled to reign as the queens of Wayward Sun Drive.

Now, Matt is dreading the day Baía is old enough to be leaving the house for romantic dates instead of play dates, but there's part of me that's looking forward to it. I'm looking forward to her learning new ways to love and be loved, and like every mother I'm hoping the lessons I've given her will serve her well. I don't know if she'll date women or men or both or neither, though I have my suspicions she'll love across lines I haven't. But whoever she loves, I hope she remembers her mother wanted her to love blackness and girlness first, second, and third: that I praised her and her friends running around the neighborhood with blue eyeshadow painted in designs on their faces, never told them to stop twerking whenever and wherever, made sure to prioritize the ways she created black-girl space for herself even if it meant children running in and out of my house slamming doors and spilling food and ruining my makeup. All black women need the support, guidance, and adoration that black femme space can provide, I think, and all of us—yes, even Beyoncé—need to seek it out at some times in our life, to come back home to the love of our own kind. Black femmes are from the future, as Che Johnson-Long hashtags, and in the future we still demand a love without betrayal that only we can give.

Calling for Freedom

BLACK WOMEN'S ACTIVISM

IN THE US SOUTH

This final part of the Femme-onade *mixtape, Beyoncé fem(me)inists, is something to accompany you on that ride to the Sister Song Women of Color Reproductive Justice Collective's national conference in New Orleans, where the title is "Let's Talk about Sex" and the theme is "Resist. Reclaim. Redefine." Or on that walk downtown to the Trans Day of Remembrance, where you know almost all the names called are going to be black trans* women's and you want to imagine a black trans* feminist song that's a celebration, not a dirge. Because sexual, reproductive, and gender freedom don't exist for black cis or trans* women in the here and now, this mixtape is for those black Southern girls who are from the future: a work song for the long, long work of demanding black feminist social change when and where we enter. 'Cause we need freedom too.*

FREEDOM, TOO

"What can we say? Like mother, like daughter!" Monika Markovinovic of Huffington Post Canada enthused the day after the 2016 Video Music Awards. "Queen of *everything, Beyoncé*, had the Internet screaming on Sunday evening when she blessed us all and brought her daughter Blue Ivy Carter onto the 2016 MTV VMAs red carpet."[1] Coordinating their jewel-toned sequined gowns, the hand-in-hand mother-daughter pair was among the first celebrities to grace the carpet that night. But "Blue wasn't Beyoncé's only date—she brought a number of women with her," MTV news noted.[2] When the paparazzi's screams overwhelmed Blue, her mother escorted her offstage and returned with a new entourage: a dozen black women and girls featured in her video "Freedom." These included Mothers of the Movement Gwen Carr, Lezley McSpadden, Sybrina Fulton, and Wanda Johnson, whose sons' racially charged murders catalyzed the Black Lives Matter movement. "The mothers of the movement always played a crucial role in Beyoncé's increasingly political advocacy," Victoria Massie reflects on *Vox*. "In the 'Forward' section of her visual album *Lemonade*, McSpadden, Fulton, and Carr are shown holding photos of their sons. Not only does Beyoncé immortalize their faces in her album, but in a kind of séance . . . a newborn baby appears alone on a bed to signal the literal and figurative transition to 'Freedom.'"[3] *Tryna rain, tryna rain on the thunder, tell the storm I'm new.*[4]

Wordlessly denouncing police brutality, Beyoncé's inter-generational legion of red-carpet companions also celebrates black women and girls' determination to mother and be mothered in the midst of *everything*—flashing cameras, failed beginnings, fallen children. "Beyoncé is fighting for a world in which black people decide their fate," Massie continues. "But it is an intergenerational struggle, as much tying black mothers to their children as it is tying the children whose lives were taken by police violence to the children who are alive today."[5] With Blue on her right and the Mothers of the Movement on her left, Beyoncé's VMA entrance embodies a call for gendered, generation-bridging black justice—for *reproductive justice*, which demands not only individuals' reproductive health but also the health of communities where black women choose to bear children. "Reproductive justice is not difficult to define or remember," Atlanta-based reproductive justice activist Loretta Ross explains. "It has three primary values: (1) the right *not* to have a child; (2) the right to *have* a child; and (3) the right to *parent* our children in safe and healthy environments. In addition, reproductive justice demands sexual autonomy and gender freedom for every human being."[6] Featuring cameos by Mothers of the Movement alongside black girls and young women like Blue, Quvenzhané Wallis, Amandla Stenberg, Zendaya, and Michaela DePrince, the cast of "Freedom" comes together to envision black women raising and nurturing daughters in just such environments. *I'ma walk, I'ma march on the regular, painting white flags blue.*[7]

When I watched Beyoncé's mother-strong arrival at the VMAs, I self-consciously did so as the mother of a black daughter in Texas—a state where black babies die and are placed in foster care at twice the rate of white infants and children. Most days, the difference between the reality of black motherhood and the ideal of reproductive justice feels as stark as the difference between Lezley McSpadden unmoved on the streets of Ferguson and moving down the red carpet. So stark that—just like Beyoncé inviting the Mothers of the Movement on the red carpet was so unprecedented I never saw it coming—it's hard for me to imagine what a world with reproductive justice for black women and girls would look like. In this chapter, I think through how "Freedom" envisions reproductive justice. But because my vision of reproductive freedom is so very, very incomplete, I can only write about it—like Beyoncé at the VMAs entering, exiting, entering again—in fits and starts, interrupted moments. My meditations on Beyoncé, Blue, Lezley, and their sisters in struggle are cut up by sketches of the reproductive justice efforts of other black women in Austin, whose experiences inform my understanding of the liberation "Freedom" demands. And they're stitched together by stories of my struggles with having children, parenting them in safe environments, and finding models for their sexual autonomy and gender freedom, stories that remind me of who we're getting free for. "To spread the reality of reproductive justice," Ross insists, we need to start paying "attention to the stories that individuals tell about their lives, including their reproductive lives" and questioning how "the opportunities and obstacles they have faced—including the ones conditioned by their families and communities—have shaped those experiences."[8] And if our communities don't support us, gather sisters to build new ones. *Freedom, freedom, where are you? 'Cause I need freedom, too!*[9]

* * *

PUBLIC JUSTICE ANNOUNCEMENT #1: MAMA SANA/VIBRANT WOMAN

Mama Sana / Vibrant Woman is a community organization that works to facilitate access to culturally appropriate and quality, prenatal and postnatal care for women of color in Austin and Travis County. Our mission: To improve pregnancy and birth outcomes for communities of color in central Texas by providing education and support. Our vision: A just and loving world.[10]

Founded in Austin in 2012, the women-of-color health project Mama Sana/Vibrant Woman produced a report titled "Austin: a Family-Friendly City, but for Whom?" in 2015. The report documented stark disparities between white and African American maternal and infant health outcomes, noting that "Black women in this city and Travis County more broadly have dangerously poor maternal health outcomes."[11] Black infant mortality rates in the county are *ten times as high* as white infant mortality rates, a gap significantly wider than state- or nationwide rates. "As a result of the racial and economic divide in Austin, Black mothers and babies are more likely to die in the childbearing year," the report concludes.[12] In response, the Austin City Council "budgeted funds for community-based, culturally specific, non-conventional health equity projects that address the systemic racial health inequities."[13] Mama Sana's current programs include pregnancy and birth circles where black and Latina mothers receive pre- and postnatal support; childbirth preparation classes led by midwives, doulas, and experienced mothers of color; wellness clinics offering checkups, homeopathy consultation, and yoga and meditation classes; and a birth companion program. Learn more about their work at https://www.msvwatx.org.

* * *

"About two years ago, I was pregnant for the first time," Beyoncé recounts in her 2013 HBO documentary *Life Is But a Dream*. She sits somberly in a handheld, low-angle close-up that tilts her image off kilter as she publicly tells the story of her miscarriage for the first time. "And I heard the heartbeat, which was the most beautiful music I ever heard in my life," she smiles sadly. "There's something that happens when you hear the heartbeat. It makes you truly know that there's *life* inside you. I picked out names. I envisioned what my child would look like. I was feeling very maternal. My *first* child, with the man I love . . . I flew back to New York to get my checkup—and no heartbeat. Literally the week before I went to the doctor, everything was fine, but there was no heartbeat." Her voice breaks as she goes on, leaving details of her miscarriage unsaid and narrating her healing instead. "I went into the studio and wrote the saddest song I've ever written in my life," she relates. "And it was the best form of therapy for me, because it was the saddest thing I've ever been through."[14] She never names the song, and references to her (possibly multiple) pregnancy losses remain veiled in her music. But many listeners hear a powerful testament to the lasting impact of miscarriage in *Lemonade*'s "Apathy," when the speaker asks her husband: "So what are you gonna say at my funeral, now that you've killed me? Here lies the body of the love of my life, whose heart I broke without a gun to my head. Here lies the mother of my children, both living and dead."[15] Citing this interlude, *Washington Post* reporter Danielle Paquette reflects: "One of the most recognizable celebrities on the planet is talking about miscarriage, a moment that could help break the stigma around the experience."[16] Twitter responded too, with Sara Cohen offering: "Grateful #Beyonce is open about #miscarriage. Real loss. Will help so many grieving."[17]

But another possible allusion to miscarriage haunted me, one that garnered less attention in the blogosphere and Twitterverse. "Hope," the poem that ushers in "Freedom," tells the story of two pregnancies: "The nail technician pushes my cuticles back, turns my hand over, stretches the skin on my palm and says, 'I see your daughters and their daughters.' That night in a dream, the first girl emerges from a slit in my stomach. The scar heals into a smile. The man I love pulls the stitches out with his fingernails."[18] In these words—"the first girl," "the man I love"—I hear echoes of Beyoncé's miscarriage in *Life Is But a Dream*: "my *first* child, with the man

I love." And the images accompanying them *look like* what miscarriage feels like. In *Grief Unseen: Healing Pregnancy Loss through the Arts*, Laura Seftel articulates why images sometimes communicate what words can't about miscarriage: "Words are not adequate to convey every human experience. Many women report that it is not easy for them to articulate the depth of emotions and physical sensations stirred up by a pregnancy loss. . . . Artist Margaret Carver turned to the creative process to express her struggle with miscarriage and infertility, 'Through art I am able to speak of an experience which is unspeakable.'"[19] As Beyoncé's voiceover narrates the first girl's emergence, the camera moves through a dark room in New Orleans's crumbling Fort Macomb that looks like Seftel's quoted description of miscarriage as a "dark little corner of women's fertility," the "reluctant underground." "The first girl emerges through a slit in my stomach," Beyoncé intones as the shot advances through a narrow, cracked (birth) passage moving toward a lit room—until the shot abruptly cuts out, the promised opening going nowhere.[20]

"The scar heals into a smile," Beyoncé's voiceover continues as the screen centers breast cancer survivor Paulette Leaphard, whose shirtless, breastless, mastectomy-scarred chest faces the camera.[21] In December 2015, Paulette took her daughter Madeline—one of eight children she raises as a single mother in Biloxi, Mississippi—to a casting call for *Lemonade*, but after telling the casting director her story she herself ended up in "Hope" instead. Her unsmiling image in a dark room of Fort Macomb visualizes trauma, loss—the loss of the living part of yourself that was closest to your heart. But dressed in the loose cotton skirt and intricate necklace of a twenty-first-century Dahomean warrior, she also visualizes resistance and survival. "I had no idea it would be this powerful," Paulette reacted to her cameo. "It was beautiful. What Beyoncé made is important. It's strong. I'm strong.

She's strong. Every woman in the video is strong. We are warriors."[22] Accessing the second principle of reproductive justice—*the right to have a child*—can be a battle for black women who are always at elevated risk for pregnancy loss even if we are as powerful as Beyoncé. "Hope" recognizes this battle and visualizes the main character emerging victorious. "I wake as the second girl crawls headfirst up my throat, a flower blossoming out of the hole in my face," the voiceover continues as Beyoncé climbs the crumbling fort walls.[23] This time, she emerges through the sunlit ceiling and blossoms onto a multigenerational, rural Southern community of black women whose abundance visualizes an ideal space to raise her daughters and daughters' daughters. A black Southern woman's version of Zion, yes, where our daughters multiply like plenty.

* * *

Zion, my love. In October 2013, I dreamed of holding a son called Zion; across the country, my mother also dreamed me with a baby boy. Zion, the promised land, heaven on earth, the place where our children will be free and always, always loved. "How beautiful if nothing more / Than to wait at Zion's door / I've never been in love like this before," Lauryn Hill sang to her unborn son Zion the year I met Matt.[24] Zion, Zion: I was barely, barely pregnant—a doctor would say, maybe, the fertilized egg had just become an embryo—and my son already told me his name in my dream. Cheeky, beautiful boy. Just before Halloween Baía and I flew to Lebanon, New Hampshire, to spend a weekend with my sister Nicole and her three children. On the plane Baía wore a custom-made Wonder Woman costume she refused to take off even in the New England fall; that Saturday I struggled to lift my four-year-old superhero out of her cousins' room to put her to bed in costume. The next morning I woke up with sharp cramps and with every one, a drop of blood squeezed between my thighs. The drops became gushes, and I realized the cramps were contractions—I was having a miscarriage. I lay in bed, watched *Paris is Burning*, rested; called my acupuncturist for a herbal prescription; prayed. But the next afternoon, just when contractions lulled and I thought they were stopping, the fetus dislodged himself with a sharp tug. I saw Zion for the first and last time as a clump on my panties. In 2010, Nicole gave birth to a stillborn son, Otis Fox, whom the family buried in their yard with an orchard planted in his memory. I hope Zion and Otis keep each other company in that orchard, resting in their own dedicated corner of heaven on earth. Zion, Zion, Zion.

I blamed myself for that miscarriage and the three that followed. Why had I lifted Baía, or done yoga on the full moon, or spent time around stressful people, or spoken about the baby? I knew pregnancy loss is an unacknowledged risk of being a reproductive female, that at least 25 percent of pregnancies end in miscarriage. What I didn't know is that pregnancy loss is a particular risk of being a black woman trying to have a child. Rates of every kind of pregnancy loss—miscarriage, stillbirth, preterm birth, infant death—are significantly higher for black women than for any other racial group. The National Institutes of Health finds that black women are twice as likely as white women to suffer late pregnancy loss and stillbirth. No genetic factors have been isolated to explain this discrepancy, and rates of loss don't vary significantly by socioeconomic status. White women with GEDs and black women with postgraduate degrees have similar rates of miscarriage. Affluent black women and working-class black women are just as likely to suffer pregnancy loss. This leads pregnancy loss expert Elizabeth Czukas to speculate "the continuous, low-grade stress of racism may be the factor that unifies all African-Americans, and may contribute to the increased risk of pregnancy loss."[25] How did carrying children in a climate of increasing violence against young black girls and boys contribute to my pregnancy losses? When I read about black children killed in churches and arrested at pools that summer, how did it affect my hormones? Did the fact that I was increasingly worried about my ability to keep my heroic daughter and future son safe have any effect on my ability to carry to term?

Zion stopped growing in my body a year after Trayvon Martin was killed in Sanford, Florida, a year before Mike Brown was gunned down in Ferguson, Missouri. In a time where too many black women are burying children in the South, the loss of my fetus seemed too intangible to merit real grief. I wasn't far along and at least I hadn't birthed a child who died after I'd gotten to know them, people told me to make me feel better. Of course, that only made me feel guilty for grieving my unborn child. So the climate of violence against black children impacted my lost pregnancies before and after the miscarriages: first made me worry about the child I was carrying, then made me feel I had no right to grieve the children I lost.

When I suffered miscarriages, my white lesbian OB-GYN told me I needed no time off. She never screened me for depression or offered information on pregnancy loss support groups. I wasn't surprised by indifference from medical professionals, really. I only learned later that white doctors may be less likely to express sympathy for black women who lose pregnancies—both because this loss is more common for us, and because we're expected to be stronger than other women, more Wonder Woman–like, less in need of consoling. But I still wanted to scream at her. I wanted to scream and sob to anyone who'd listen that women like me, black mothers, we're not breeders. We're not superwomen. We're as fragile and resilient as anyone else; we deserve to be taken care of by people who reflect back that our stories of love and loss are meaningful; we deserve to bear and lose children in communities of support. *Unsure of what the balance held / I touched my belly overwhelmed / By what I had been chosen to perform.*[26] Zion, my baby.

* * *

PUBLIC JUSTICE ANNOUNCEMENT #2: THE EXCELLENCE AND ADVANCEMENT FOUNDATION

The goals of The Excellence and Advancement Foundation are: to focus public attention on the criminalization process that impacts our children, to help challenge the various agencies, individuals, and organizations that work with both these children and adults, to come together to break the cycle of incarceration . . . There are a variety of systems (Educational, Justice, and Child Welfare) contributing to incarceration. We challenge systems to reevaluate how they handle children.[27]

In Texas, Child Protective Services removes African American children from homes at twice the rate of white children. The Texas Department of Family and Protective Services acknowledges on its website: "African American children comprised 11.6% of the general child population of Texas but accounted for almost 28.0% of all children awaiting adoption.[28] Even when other factors are taken into account, African American children spend more time in foster care, or other substitute care, are less likely to go home to their parents, and wait longer for adoption."[29] Foster care is *not* a safe and healthy environment for these children. Texas-based Arrow Child and Family Ministries' 2016 report finds that 80 percent of the prison population was once in foster care, and girls in foster care are 600 percent more likely than the general population to become pregnant before age twenty-one. The Excellence and Advancement Foundation attempts to prevent black children in foster care from going to jail or losing their own children to foster care by offering an enrichment program for third through twelfth graders "to improve racial identity, help children and their parents discover the depth and breadth of Black history, improve academic engagement, college readiness and community engagement"; it offers individualized service plans for black children caught in the criminal justice or school discipline systems at its Excellence Resource Center. Read about their expanding programs at http://breakthepipeline.com.

* * *

"Freedom! Freedom! I can't move / Freedom, cut me loose! / Freedom! Freedom! Where are you? / 'Cause I need freedom too!"[30] A black-and-white dream vision of the rural antebellum South, "Freedom" lovingly gathers an imaginary community of black women and girls—featuring cameos by activists, actresses, singers, and dancers from around the diaspora— who sway shoulder to shoulder at a candlelit church revival and pass each other heaping dishes at a sumptuous outdoor repast. "When we started we were thinking about antebellum South, and Bey was talking about going back to these plantations," *Lemonade* stylist Marni Senofonte explains the video's look. "There was a question of, 'Do we do authentic vintage or is it about wearing couture on these plantations?' And I was like, 'It's about wearing couture on these plantations!' You have fifty amazing women in there and Bey was in couture Givenchy up in the tree. It's a juxtaposition of what historically black women on a plantation were."[31] In Beyoncé's video, too, twenty-first-century black women are still living in the era of slavery—but from the same plantations where they were enslaved, mothers, daughters, and sisters sing for their freedom. *Freedom, freedom, where are you?*

Deliberately historically unrealistic, "Freedom" still keeps faithful to the spirit of black church revivals in the slavery-era South. "In the crowds that attended the revivals and camp meetings there were numbers of Negroes who found in the fiery message of salvation a hope and a prospect of escape from their earthly woes," E. Franklin Frazier notes in his classic *The Negro Church in America*. "The slaves, who had been torn from their homeland and kinsmen and friends and whose cultural heritage was lost, were isolated and broken men, so to speak. In the emotionalism of the camp meetings and revivals some social solidarity, even if temporary, was achieved, and they were drawn into a union with their fellow men."[32] The revival of "Freedom," though, celebrates the main character's union with *sister women*. Black women and girls "need freedom too," Beyoncé sings, and orchestrates a lavish vision of what it would look like if we were free to mother each other and ourselves in grace and abundance: because for black women, there is no freedom without "the right to nurture the children we have in safe and healthy environments."[33] The power of black women being able to mother biological, adoptive, and fictive kin encompasses "far more than an individual's reproductive decision making," Loretta Ross explains. "Mothering is an act of survival, a life-affirming radical resistance to forces that deny our humanity, our interdependence, and even our existence," she holds forth. "Radical mothers withstand oppression to create spaces for life. . . . How we imagine and describe different or better futures is a core concern of reproductive justice, which asks, can we stop the injuries long enough to even envision the remedies?"[34] Sing, Beyoncé, sing: "I break chains all by myself / Won't let my freedom rot in hell / Hey! I'ma keep running / 'Cause a winner don't quit on themselves."[35]

Singing a cappella on a candlelit wooden stage, Beyoncé stands as the revival preacher for her "Freedom" congregation. But she disappears after the first chorus and is replaced onstage by ballerina Michaela DePrince, who soulfully soloes wearing a white vintage dress, flower crown, and signature brown pointe shoes. Born in 1995 in Sierra Leone, four-year-old Michaela was adopted by white Americans Elaine and Charles DePrince after her mother died of fever and starvation in the bed they shared. When Elaine met her in an orphanage, she carried her most prized possession in her underwear: the cover of a 1979 issue of *Dance* magazine featuring a smiling white dancer en pointe. "It was not just the fact that she's a ballerina. It's that she looks happy. And I wanted to be happy," Michaela remembers. "If what she was doing made her happy, that's what I wanted to do."[36] "I couldn't believe that I had adopted an orphan from Africa who wanted pointe shoes!" Elaine adds. "I had to promise her . . . she would dance."[37] When Michaela braved professional ballet's racism to become Dance Theater of Harlem's youngest dancer and a principal in the Dutch National Ballet at eighteen, her adoption story became a media flashpoint. "There were many articles that criticized the way our adoptions had been handled. The adoptions were described as human trafficking, and worse. In a blog an American activist said that we might have been better off with our birth parents," Michaela writes in her autobiography.[38] While Michaela found a fiercely protective and loving mother in Elaine, the global inequalities that leave women in Sierra Leone vulnerable to dying young—and white women in the global north in positions to more safely raise their children—loom large in her story. "Contemporary international adoption, having flown in almost half a million children to Western countries during a period of fifty years, has parallels to the Atlantic slave trade—which between 1510 and 1870 shipped eleven million Africans to the New World," Tobias

Hübinette notes. "I conceptualize international adoption as a mixed project of colonial uplifting, civilizing, and assimilating non-Western children" into white families.[39]

But center stage at the revival in "Freedom," Michaela dances for a whole community of loving, justice-seeking black mothers. Seated in the front pew watching her are Lezley McSpadden, Gwen Carr, and Sybrina Fulton. Pushed to the forefront of the Black Lives Matter movement in the wake of their sons' murders, these women were sisters in struggle long before they were cast together in *Lemonade*. "The mothers I've met along the way—Sybrina Fulton, Trayvon Martin's mother; Wanda Johnson, Oscar Grant III's mother—we've helped one another cope," Lezley reflects. "When their children are killed, mothers are expected to say something. To help keep the peace. To help make change. But what can I possibly say?"[40] Seated in the front pew looking both gentle and regal—"I got there and they wanted to make me look regal. That's what [Beyoncé] called it," Lezley recalls[41]—these mothers aren't called on to *say* anything. They are there listening, there for revival: "a time where old, decaying situations are rejuvenated with life, where people . . . are renewed and inspired," as Marla Frederick describes black church revivals in rural North Carolina.[42] Renewal, yes: because at this revival all black mothers who have lost sons are surrounded by loving black children, *again*, and all black children who have lost mothers are surrounded by a community of black matriarchs, *again*. When asked the highlights of working on *Lemonade*, Michaela described its intergenerational family of black women: "I talked with the mothers [who were] present [on set] . . . but best of all, I talked to Blue Ivy. . . . She reminded me of my niece."[43]

"I could not have been happier to participate in [Beyoncé's project]. And how great to dance to the song, 'Freedom,'" Michaela reflects. "The director gave me music to listen to,

and about three minutes later, he had me dance to it. I improvised, choreographing the dance on the spot."[44] The perfectly
extended arabesques, pas de bourrés, and high-V and asym-
metrical arm movements of her choreography recall Odette's
variation from *Swan Lake*: one of the most canonical ballets
of all time, yes, but also a story of mothers' pain at being separated from their children. Odette, a princess turned into a
swan by an evil sorcerer she refuses to marry, lives and dances
on an enchanted lake filled by her inconsolable mother's tears.
"I'm telling these tears go and fall away, fall away / May the
last one burn into flames," Beyoncé sings to Michaela's choreography.[45] Spirit has spoken, sisters, let the church say amen.
And the prayer at Beyoncé and Michaela's revival just might
be the third principle of reproductive justice: *may all black
women be free to "parent our children in safe and healthy environments."*[46] Let your lake burn into flames, swan princess, so you
can return to your beloved community of mothers and sisters
who love you.

* * *

The weekend of Mother's Day 2017, Baía, Matt, and I found
ourselves flying into a hard-blossoming New Hampshire spring
so I could give a talk at Dartmouth. On a whim, we decided
to drive down to Massachusetts to spend the holiday with
my grandmother and cousins. I coordinated details with my
cousin Laura, expressing my special hope that her sister Anna
and her two daughters—Zoey, five, and Maya, two—could
celebrate with us. Born when I was a junior in high school,
Anna wasn't a cousin I grew up playing with. I remember her
at funerals, our grandfather's when she was six and her mother's when she was thirteen; at weddings, beautiful at my sister
Christina's when she was seventeen; and chatting at my grandparents' kitchen table every visit I made. Though we weren't

close growing up, I share with Anna something I can't share with any of my grandparents' other granddaughters: of the five of us, Anna and I are the only two who can't pass—the only two who move through the world as black women. When my lighter-skinned sisters had blonde children and I had Baía, the concerns, joys, and day-to-day hair-doing and ash-lotioning of being a black mother were things I couldn't share with them. But I wanted to see Anna and her daughters, partly, because maybe she'd be the one person in my family who could really understand what it feels like to be a black mother who, in the midst of too much judgment and too little respect, wants to raise her daughters on love and possibility.

Laura told me Anna probably wouldn't make it for Mother's Day but didn't tell me why. When we were leaving, I casually mentioned I wished Baía could've met Zoey and Maya, and my grandmother—a woman so stoic she apologized for crying at her husband's funeral—broke into tears. Zoey and Maya hadn't been living with Anna for months, she told me, because when she and her boyfriend lost their apartment the girls were placed in foster care with two different white families. I was floored: two little girls separated from their mother and each other, too, just because they're working poor? In *Shattered Bonds: The Color of Child Welfare*, Dorothy Roberts documents black children's stark overrepresentation in the foster care system where "the proportion of Black children in out-of-home care in large states such as California, Illinois, and Texas ranges from three times to more than ten times the proportion as high as the proportion of white children."[47] Like Anna, black mothers most often have their children taken not because of abuse or addiction, but because the child welfare system criminalizes lack of adequate income and housing as threats to children's safety. "Inadequate housing is frequently at the center of caseworkers' decisions to place children in foster care," Roberts reports. "The US Department of Health and Human Services reports that children from families with housing problems are more likely to stay in the system longer. Children are routinely kept in foster care because their parents are unable to find decent affordable housing."[48] When I frantically texted Anna to find out what was going on with Zoey and Maya, she explained no matter how closely she follows her case plan the state refuses to return her girls until she finds an apartment she can afford in the overpriced suburban Boston market. "My social worker flat out told us we have the best potential as parents of any people she has ever worked with," she texted. "They had everything they ever needed. What's in the best interest of the kids doesn't matter."

Parental rights attorneys call poor black women's extreme vulnerability to losing their children "Jane Crow," citing the racialized "power of Children's Services to take children" from black mothers who have too few resources and criminalize their poverty "on the grounds that the child's safety is at risk, even with scant evidence."[49] "The hardest part," Anna wrote me, "is almost every person who hears that you have lost your babies thinks that you are a terrible person and that you must have done something to deserve it. No one understands just how easy it can be to lose your kids until it happens to you or a loved one." It *can* happen to any black woman, including the mother of one of the most brilliant leaders of the twentieth century. In his autobiography, Malcolm X recounts his experience in the child welfare system after his mother's stress-induced breakdown, and calls the forced removal of children from black mothers to white foster families "legal, modern slavery—however kindly intentioned."[50] "Sometimes I feel like we're not that far from slavery, when black women's kids could be taken at any time," I texted Anna before I remembered Malcolm's words. After all these years and all this love, Anna, we're still not free. But may Zoey and Maya be freed from the system to come home for good.

* * *

PUBLIC JUSTICE ANNOUNCEMENT #3: ALLGO

Allgo: a statewide queer people of color organization celebrates and nurtures vibrant queer people of color communities in Texas and beyond. We do this through cultural arts, wellness, and social justice programming by: supporting artists and artistic expression within our diverse communities; promoting health within a wellness model; and mobilizing and building coalitions among groups marginalized by race/ethnicity, gender/gender identity, sexual orientation/sexual identity in order to enact change.[51]

The day after we moved to Austin, Matt, Baía, and I went to a Christmas party hosted by allgo at the beautiful house of director Priscilla Hale. Baía came in one of the Capezio tutus she insisted on wearing every day that winter and danced her version of ballet alongside other black and brown children and their gay aunties, uncles, mamas, and grandmas getting down to old-school Michael Jackson and slow jams. This was the first allgo party Baía and I attended—the first of many. At every allgo event, serving queer people of color includes serving our children: because, proud grandmother Priscilla is clear, there's no justice without their participation. "It cannot be stated enough how important it is for QPOC youth and QPOC elders to be able to interact and spend time with each other," the allgo blog lays out. "The ability to see people who are not only living similar experiences as you, but are thriving, strong and growing can shape the way a person approaches their life experiences. . . . The ability for youth and their parents to participate in community events will not only make events better, but will create a space where communities are able to truly come together as a whole."[52] Support their work at http://allgo.org/.

* * *

Weak-kneed as I was (and am) watching Serena twerk on Queen Bey in "Sorry," "Freedom" slowly took its place as my favorite *Lemonade* video. The reason I love it is simple: its dream of black feminist freedom made flesh always plays, to me, like a public declaration of love and hope for the woman Blue Ivy will become. Blue is the youngest actress featured in "Freedom." Her memorable cameo finds the Afro-haloed, white-clad preschooler standing with eyes cast down under a tree at Madewood Plantation, hand in hand with twelve-year-old actress Quvenzhané Wallis. "Won't let my freedom rot in hell," Beyoncé croons fiercely over their shot.[53] Never helpless children, Blue, Quvenzhané, and all black youth in "Freedom" also come to break chains all by themselves: to model what reproductive justice activists' call for "sexual autonomy and gender freedom for every human being" looks like for black girls, coming into reproductive maturity in the shadows of misogynoir.[54]

Wearing a dress similar to Beyoncé's as she gazes steadily at the camera, Quvenzhané looks like Blue's knowing, protective older sister. In 2013, Quvenzhané became the youngest actor and first person born this century to be nominated for an Academy Award. When the nine-year-old attended the Oscars wearing a royal blue dress and sparkly headband, carrying a puppy purse, Kelly Osbourne called her "Little Q" instead of trying to pronounce her name and satirical newspaper *The Onion* tweeted as a "joke": "Everyone else seems afraid to say it, but that Quvenzhané Wallis is kind of a cunt, right?"[55] The blogosphere erupted with outrage. In her piece "On Being A Little Black Girl in the World: For Quvenzhané Wallis," Black

Girl Dangerous blogger Mia McKenzie reflects: "The thing about being a little black girl in the world is that your right to be a child, to be small and innocent and protected, will be ignored and you will be seen as a tiny adult, a tiny black adult, and as such will be susceptible to all the offenses that people two and three and four times your age are expected to endure."[56] Adultification and hypersexualization represent one of the earliest threats to sexual autonomy for girls like Quvenzhané and Blue, Corinne and Baía. "At the same time that black girls are oversexualized and considered sexually aberrant in the media, black women are infantilized, viewed as play things who are endlessly sexually available and childlike," Sika Dagbovie-Mullins writes. "The prevalence and acceptance of these damaging images . . . suggests that black girls aren't really girls. The dangerous entangling of woman and girl prompts us to think about black girls in two interrelated and degrading ways: they are forgettable and invisible and yet highly visible, hypersexual, and repelling."[57]

But holding hands with Blue in "Freedom," Quvenzhané is where she belongs: a child with other children, protected and protective, getting free. "The thing about being a little black girl in the world is that you will be surrounded by other black girls who know. And they will hold your hand and braid your hair and laugh with you. They will tell you that you are a gift. They will let you be perfect and let you be flawed. They will rock you in their arms and protect your heart," McKenzie's tribute to Quvenzhané continues. "Some of them will even help you get free."[58] Another shot of Quvenzhané places her in front of an ornate mirror inside the plantation great house, lit by the flame of ascending candles and staring over her shoulder at her poised reflection. This black girl creates and projects *her own* image of herself and her beauty, shining like natural light at night.

Blue also meets a second sister figure in "Freedom," seated in the branches of the tree that frames her and Quvenzhané's cameo. When Amandla Stenberg answered Beyoncé's call to shoot scenes for *Lemonade*, Queen Bey made the reason behind her invitation clear: "When Blue grows up, I want her to be just like you." "I felt like the hands of God were, like, gently caressing my entire body and soul, like I felt like I had reached nirvana, and I was like, 'Thank you very much,'" Amandla laughingly describes her reaction.[59] Amandla earned her reputation as "wokest teenager alive" after her 2015 video "Don't Cashcrop my Cornrows"—which launches the pointed question "What would America be like if we loved black people as much as we love black culture?"—went viral.[60] Subsequently courted for magazine interviews and talks, she's been consistently outspoken about her black feminist and queer self-identifications. "I don't think gender even exists," she tells *Vogue*. "My sexuality's very fluid and my gender is very fluid. I don't think of myself as statically a girl."[61] Her treetop "Freedom" cameo is electric with queer subtext: seated side by side on a branch with fellow teen actor Zendaya, sunlight and Spanish moss cascading down their backs, their shot pays homage to a scene in Julie Dash's film *Daughters of the Dust* in which protagonist Yellow Mary and her lover Trula perch in a majestic tree to tell their story.

Beyoncé's choice to provide an openly queer role model for Blue—whose paternal grandmother Gloria Carter is a lesbian—is a quiet but powerful statement. "For the queer black kids, queer in all kinds of ways, including but not limited to different, gay, quirky, dykey, and fabulous, who are learning right now . . . that there is shame in not being small enough to fit neatly into a box marked boy or girl," Mia McKenzie declares: "We know how confusing it is when people talk about wanting you to be free, and then do everything they can to keep you from being free. We know what it is to wonder how freedom could possibly look like just the same old box."[62] No, *no*, the freedom Beyoncé imagines for Blue looks nothing like that. No wooden box, her freedom is a tree of life: a transatlantic revision of the African baobab, which flourishes for millennia in the arid savannah and whose leaves mothers mix into babies' baths to help them grow strong and big. *That*, y'all, is reproductive justice made real.

* * *

Mothers aren't supposed to have favorites among their children's friends, I suppose, but it's hard to help. One Saturday when I was reading Dorothy Roberts's *Shattered Bonds* and thinking about Zoey and Maya, Baía's friend Corinne—the only other black girl in her class in second grade, whom she started a short-lived perfume business with—came for a play date. The girls retreated to her room for a while, then paraded into the living room with arms full of black baby dolls. In their game, they explained, they were a married couple who had thirteen daughters and one son and were both pregnant again, Corinne with quadruplets and Baía with quintuplets. They asked if I'd play Baía's mother (easily) and complain about their ever-multiplying family. I did, and for every objection I made they had an instant answer: yes, they had a big enough house the size of a whole block and yes, they could feed everyone at once by putting all the food in the middle of the table and letting the babies take what they want and yes, they had two vans for everyone to ride in and yes, they were happy to be pregnant at the same time and feeling great.

I loved that game because of the girls' amazing certainty in the possibilities of abundance for black mothers and daughters, their faith in black women and girls' ability to create and sustain life with endless love. And I loved it because it was a

Corinne, Baía, and a few of their babies.
Photograph by Matt Richardson.

game I never, ever would have come up with at that age. In the first place, the idea that two black women could fall in love, get married, and have as many children as they wanted together was something I simply didn't know was possible. But as the oldest of four children by Corinne's age, the idea that twenty-three children could live happily under one roof and want for nothing was something I would've dismissed as even less realistic than the princess games I'd just grown out of. And now here in my living room were two black girls raised in Texas—the state with the nation's highest maternal mortality for black women, the state whose supreme court unanimously ruled same-sex married couples aren't guaranteed the same spousal benefits as straight couples—with a clear vision of what reproductive freedom could, should, and would look like for them. Thank you, Corinne and Baía. May you and all the indigo children inherit the earth and love it black, feminist, and queer to the future. *I'm a rain, I'm a rain on this bitter love / Tell the sweet I'm new.*[63]

I CAME TO SLAY

"Slay bitch, *what*. Slay bitch, *what*. Slay, slay, slay, bitch *what*. I'm a Southern girl in a Southern world. I like corn breads and collard greens, bitch," Big Freedia spits into the mike on the episode of her reality show titled "Omg it's Beyoncé!"[1] Homegrown New Orleans sissy from Josephine Street and Queen of Bounce, you already know: this queer "Southern girl in a Southern world," whose success helped popularize bounce music nationwide and whose top-rated show *Big Freedia, Queen of Bounce* brings black LGBT life to millions of viewers, projects a public voice for black New Orleans music and black gender freedom everywhere she goes. "I want people to be able to identify as whomever they choose to be and feel free to be whomever they want to be," she tells the *Advocate* about gender identity[2] and explains her preferred pronouns are "whatever you choose, he or she. I'm confident and know who I am. . . . I usually go with 'she' most of the time, but if somebody say 'he' I'm like 'what's up, bro.'"[3] Earlier in "Omg it's Beyoncé!" Freedia is in a tiger-print bathrobe cooking gumbo when a surprise call startles the spatula out of her hand. It's Beyoncé, asking if the Queen of Bounce is available to record a few lines for her new song "Formation." The song is about reclaiming her Louisiana heritage, Bey explains, proclaiming "no matter how big she get or whatever, she still just gonna be a black Southern girl"; she wants Freedia to contribute a New Orleans–style hook about "slaying, you know," because "she's slaying on this track." "Queen Bee and Queen Free!" Freedia proudly titles their collaboration just before she steps up to record.[4]

Beyoncé's surprise release of the "Formation" video came days after Freedia laid down her part on the track, immediately garnering millions of views, thousands of think pieces, and endless dances of joy. "Formation" is *Lemonade*'s beginning, the only song and video released prior to the film's debut; and also *Lemonade*'s end point, the final track and last stop on the main character's path to healing. Its video is a New Orleans–style celebration of all things black, womanly, and Southern: women and girls with parasols and hot sauce getting in formation in a Storyville hotel, a plantation big house, a hair shop, a parking lot, a church—a whole Southern world where they enjoy their bodies in all their blackness and womanness. Inviting Freedia—the album's only LGBT featured artist—to join this black women's power anthem queers *Lemonade*'s homage to black Southern womanhood as its finishing flourish. Queen Bee and Queen Free join voices to celebrate the art of black femininity in *every* body brave enough to "dream it . . . work hard . . . grind 'til" you "own it."[5] As Zandria Robinson writes: "'Formation' is an homage to and recognition of the werk of the 'punks, bulldaggers, and welfare queens' in these Southern streets and parking lots, in these second lines, in these chocolate cities and neighborhoods, in front of these bands and drumlines."[6]

Images of water literally flood "Formation," which begins and ends with Beyoncé singing on the hood of a police car sinking into waters that recall Hurricane Katrina. Filmed in New Orleans, *Big Freedia, Queen of Bounce* also features numerous shots of the city's waters—from an image of the Mississippi just before Freedia's call with Beyoncé to a flashback to Freedia's escape from the city after Katrina. Footage of the city buffeted by the storm and refugees lining a freeway flyover rolls as Freedia gives her publicist a tour of the path she followed to evacuate after Katrina: "Look, all this Katrina. Completely gutted. This whole house was underwater. Trees was knocked all down, power lines. The boat came and rescued us. The boat let us out right here by the bridge.

We all slept on this bridge right here for a few days."[7] Powerful enough to take life and give it back again, wateriness is the element that joins Beyoncé's and Freedia's visions of black feminine folk in the South—literally and also figuratively. In "We Got Issues: Toward a Black Trans*/Studies," my husband Matt Richardson and friends Treva Ellison, Kai Greene, and C. Riley Snorton imagine the connections between canonical black feminism and black transfeminism as fluid, slippery, mobile like "submarine roots" that are "floating free, not fixed in one position . . . but extending in all directions . . . [in a] shared process of cultural mutation . . . that frees us from uniformity."[8] Or to put it in Louisiana terms, cis and trans* ways of being "a Southern girl in a Southern world" are like the waters of a bayou: interweaving channels that converge to slow a river's flow, creating an environment where abundant, diverse life forms evolve and thrive. But never underestimate the watery power of this black feminist bayou, y'all. Because like a swamp whose alligators and floods take out those who don't respect its boundaries, black and trans* women in formation can force the world to change.

The current that draws black trans* and cis women into "Formation" rides on the word Beyoncé asks Freedia to riff off—*slay*. "To be on point, to win, to be outstanding, or to be the best," per RuPaul's Drag Race Dictionary,[9] "slay" comes to popular culture from queer-of-color ballroom competitions where "slaying and snatching"—beating competitors and winning trophies in drag contests—marks individual and collective success for trans* women and gay men whose blackness, femininity, and power too often go uncelebrated. "Within the Ballroom social sphere, where its members do not enjoy a wide range of intimacy with their biological families, Ballroom houses offer a space for care, service, competition, and critique among people who share similar life experiences,"

Marlon Bailey explains. "Not only is this bond drawn on characteristics of kin, but it is based on a common drive to 'slay and snatch' trophies for a house,'" so that "bonding, 'slaying and snatching,' and building a kin network" become interwoven processes.[10] Ciscentric black gender common sense might imagine that trans★ women measure their success by cis women—that "slaying" means acting as much like a cis woman as possible. But in "Formation," Freedia's black transfemininity sets the standard for slaying: she introduces the word to the song before Beyoncé builds her chorus around it, suggesting that to "be on point, to win, to be outstanding, or to be the best"—to *get in formation*—cis women need to follow trans★ sisters' examples of art, activism, and community-building. And the love, joy, and pride that surround Queen Bee and Queen Free's collaboration models possibilities for what transinclusive black feminism could *feel like*. "Love you too, honey," Freedia says as she gets off the phone with Beyoncé, and Freedia's Uncle Percy declares: "Your mama would be so proud of you."[11] *Oh yes you besta believe it*, black Southern trans★ and cis women slaying together makes our heavenly mothers proud.

✳ ✳ ✳

You're my lifeline, are you tryna kill me?[12] "Formation" dropped in February 2016, a month into the deadliest year on record for North American trans★ folk. When Monica Loera was shot to death near our North Austin home on January 22, her murder became the first of the nation's twenty-seven trans★ homicides and the first of Texas's four transfemicides. Matt and I were living in a state that *again* led the United States in trans★ murders, and every morning I logged onto social media praying not to find a black trans★ woman's picture captioned

"Missing" or "Rest in Power." I never bother checking mainstream or African American news outlets for that kind of information, since both still underreport and misreport violence against black trans* women. In spite of the fact that trans* women of color were being murdered at a rate of almost one per week in the United States at the time "Formation" came out. And the fact that the Southern Poverty Law Center documents trans* women of color are the group most victimized by hate crimes. And the fact that almost 70 percent of victims of anti-LGBT murders are trans* women of color. And that Houston's black State Representative Garnet Coleman argued that "transgender individuals in the US have a one-in-twelve chance of being murdered" when he unsuccessfully urged Texas to add violence against trans* folk to its list of hate crimes in 2015.[13]

So by February 2016, I was *thirsty*. As the wife of a black transman who worries for my husband's safety when he's not home on time; as the mother of a black daughter who wants her to grow up in a world where her father's gender is something to celebrate; as the friend of black trans* folk I know as not as statistics but as people who like flaming hot Cheetos or don't, people who go to church or don't, people who prefer "Formation" to "Flawless***" or don't, people who rock electric color hair or don't: I was thirsty as fuck for images that black trans* lives matter. That yes, black trans* women and men have the divine right to be creative and joyful with their bodies and lives, and black trans* folk slay more often than they are slain. Because the only events more criminally underreported than black trans* women's deaths are their lives; and by the time *Lemonade* dropped, we were living in a Texas-harsh media drought of images of reflecting black trans* women's complex, carefree and careful lives. *Make it rain now, stop this love drought.*[14]

* * *

The day after the 2017 Grammys, Laverne Cox revealed how *Lemonade* came *this close* to featuring two black trans★ divas. Laverne finally met her longtime idol at the awards show, and their meeting was everything the black trans★ actress and activist dreamed of. "She sees me and her face lights up. My god. Awe. And she says can somebody help me up? And she didn't get up for anybody else. But I was like, my god. I'll help you up," Laverne told *Essence*. "And so Beyoncé gets up for me then she gives me a big hug. Awe. Awe. And she was like I love you so much. And I was like I love you. Love you so much and I just thank you and congratulations."[15] Laverne also revealed that the two almost met a year earlier when she was approached to appear in *Lemonade*. "Miss Tina contacted me about their initial concept of 'Sorry' from *Lemonade*," Laverne explained. "They wanted to have all these powerful, empowered black women in the video and they wanted to have me and Viola [Davis] and Kerry [Washington]."[16] But Laverne—busy that year starring in two television shows and a remake of *Rocky Horror Picture Show*—regretfully declined, graciously recognizing that Serena Williams proved "perfect" for the video. Once she wrapped up her demanding shooting schedule, Laverne consoled herself with a week-long trip to St. Maarten. There she posted a stunning picture of herself in a cherry-red monokini standing in the island's turquoise waters and captioned it "#TransIsBeautiful." "It was just divine to be around nature and experience the majesty of God," she told *Watch!* magazine. "For me, when I'm near the ocean and can hear the water and feel the breeze, that's heaven."[17]

Like Freedia and Beyoncé, Laverne is a black Southern girl. Growing up in Mobile, Alabama, with her mother and twin brother, she was a straight-A student who never managed to fit in. "As a child I knew everyone was telling me that I was a boy but I felt like a girl. I thought I would hit puberty and just start turning into a girl," she remembers.[18] When Laverne was eight, "my third grade teacher called my mother and said, 'Ms. Cox, your son is going to end up in New Orleans in a dress if we don't get him into therapy.'"[19] And sure enough, Laverne ended up in New Orleans and most major Southern cities wearing a dress—fabulously styled as she toured the country with her speech "Ain't I a Woman?" Speaking at the University of Kentucky, she opened recounting her third-grade teacher's worry and quipping: "And wouldn't you know, just last week I spoke at Tulane University, and I wore a LOVELY green and black dress."[20] Years before her idol Beyoncé, Laverne publicly and proudly claimed the title of black feminist. Her feminist consciousness evolved from growing up seeing her working-class mother's challenges in the Deep South, she remembers, and the unapologetic blackness of her feminism came from being raised in a state central to the civil rights movement. She's as crystal clear as St. Maarten's waters that black transfeminist and cisfeminist politics flow together, and that to miss their crosscurrents is to fail black women. "Trans rights are women's rights," she commented at the *Essence* Black Women in Hollywood Awards. "Part of what's so exciting about being at this event tonight is that I'm a black trans woman. I'm a woman but I'm also trans. It's about always including trans voices in discussions about women's rights."[21]

Laverne's activism takes many forms, from educating viewers on mainstream media shows, to public campaigns against the disproportionate incarceration of trans★ women of color, to protests against anti-trans★ bathroom laws. All are powered by her belief in black trans★ love: because, as Laverne writes, "justice is what love looks like in public."[22] Giving the keynote address at the 2014 Trans 100, she radiated: "This feels so amazing, all this love that you're giving me tonight. I have to say that a black, transgender woman from a working-class background raised by a single mother—that's me—getting all this love tonight—this feels like the change I need to see more of in this country . . . Trans women supporting and loving each other is a revolutionary act."[23] And African America supporting and loving trans* women is a revolutionary act, too. "Black America, my brothers and sisters, I love you and claim you," she declares in "Ain't I a Woman?" "Do you love and claim me as the black woman I am?"[24] So when Beyoncé appreciated Laverne's *Lip Synch Battle* performance by sending four potted orchids—symbols of womanhood—and a handwritten note that read "Laverne, Thank you for blessing this world with your slayage. You were gorgeous on *Lip Sync Battle*. Love, Beyoncé," and Laverne answered with ten heart emojis: their public declaration of love was black Southern feminism in action.[25] Black daughters of Alabama negroes gotta stick together, y'all.

* * *

"I did not come to play with you hoes, hahaha. I came to slay, bitch," Freedia's voiceover booms over a single plucked sitar a minute into "Formation."[26] As the final sitar note punctuates the end of the line, the video cuts—first to a shot of women's feet in slides that read UH HUH HONEY—then to a medium close-up of a chocolate-skinned woman with cascading teal hair who stares evenly back at viewers. The camera eventually pans to a full-body shot of these women standing shoulder to shoulder with a third, posed like the black Three Graces in the aisle of a hair store where shelves of wigs frame their stance. "Oh yes, you besta believe it," Freedia delivers her signature line as the middle Grace combs the wig she holds in her hand.[27] Like *Lemonade*'s other featured artists, Freedia doesn't appear on camera in the video. But the impact of not including The Weeknd or Kendrick Lamar in the film isn't the same as passing Freedia over. "Given Big Freedia's sonic vivification on 'Formation,' a visual text that is a part of Beyoncé's celebration of the majesty, strength, and beauty of black women that enlivens the visual album *Lemonade*, it is curious that Beyoncé chose not to feature Big Freedia's body in the video along with the renowned voice," my black femme colleague Jennifer DeClue points out. "The history of transwomen in feminist circles or within gay and lesbian communities has been fraught with exclusion and contested admission . . . [and] an absent presence is produced when the sonic incorporation of Big Freedia's voice is met by the visual occlusion of Big Freedia's body."[28] I love Big Freedia and would have been overjoyed to see her in "Formation"—to witness Beyoncé make a strong transinclusive black feminist statement with Queen Free's screen time. But giving Freedia the phrase that anchors the song, *I came to slay*, and linking that phrase to the hair shop, imagines another kind of black trans★ and cis sisterhood, one as complicated and simple as a weave.

Hair stores—where you can purchase wigs, extensions, and other hairstyling products—and hair shops—where those wigs and extensions are turned into your latest style—are touchstones for black Southern women, places where transfeminine and cisfeminine folk come together to create beauty, meet friends, and talk about days, loves, and lives. As Willi Coleman lyricizes, the black hair shop is "a place where extraordinary cultural, political and economic business [gets] taken care of": "Ya could meet / A whole lot of other women / Sittin there . . . / Lots more got taken care of / than hair . . . / We came together / Under the hot comb / To share / And share / And / Share."[29] And it's also a place where black cis- and trans★ women work together to coproduce womanhood. In 2009, Freedia starred in the New Orleans bounce musical *Catch*

Dat Beat as a transfeminine hairdresser working in a shop where "Freedia's customers, mostly women, come to get their hair done and, while waiting, recount their own experiences with Bounce music while lambasting each other over hair, style, and who Freedia's going to work on next," according to Alix Chapman.[30] This staged scene mirrors the everyday importance of doing hair for black transfeminine folk in New Orleans, as Chapman documents in his dissertation on black gay men and transwomen in bounce. Black transfeminine and cisfeminine folk depend on each other in New Orleans in ways Chapman sees crystallized in the process of getting hair did: since most of the transfeminine "Bounce performers I worked with made their livings as beauticians, and stylists, supplementing their careers as entertainers with work in other informal economies as well. Black gay men and trans people tended to perform cultural labor as stylists and entertainers, while straight and queer members of the black community comprised both audience and clients."[31]

Chapman describes in loving detail an afternoon spent waiting to get his hair cut by Jun, a queer bounce artist working out of his grandmother's hot kitchen that day. "Jun, myself, and a group of black women discussed the meanings of blackness, sexuality, and gender . . . in an exercise of self-definition," Chapman remembers, and "the dialogue between Jun's clients and I were associated with our shared desire to create meanings of space and blackness counter to masculinist and heteronormative social relationships."[32] Hairstyling is an attractive profession (literally and figuratively) for folk like Jun because it's a business with low startup costs where black transfeminine folks' skill set and gender presentation are provided their own material space—the (makeshift) hair shop, maybe carved out of space black grandmothers, aunties, or sisters share—to develop and flourish. But it's also attractive because along with the styling of women's bodies (cis- and transfeminine alike), Jun and his clients are perform-ing the cultural and conceptual work of *working through* wom-anhood, exploring what it can mean to themselves and their sister-friends. What Ginetta Candelario writes of New York's Dominican beauty salons also rings true for Jun's grand-mother's kitchen: "While beauty regimes are not empower-ing [for women of African descent], the community that is developed around beauty practices often is. Small revolutions ferment in the beauty shop daily when Dominican women confront oppressive conditions generated by government of-fices, hospitals, schools, employers, husbands, and lovers, with the support and assistance of beauty shop kin."[33]

Yes, for all that getting hair and doing hair means to black trans* and cis sisterhood, pairing Freedia's voiceover with the endless styling possibilities of the hair store *means something* in New Orleans queer culture. But my favorite part about the wig-loving (cis? trans*?) Graces of "Formation" is the teal color hair of the actress captured in medium close-up. Her saturated aquamarine tresses look like the mermaid hair pop-ularized by singer Azealia Banks (and coopted by Kylie Jenner): a fantastical look that imagines black women *are* magic, that the art of being a black woman is turning ourselves into god-desses and sirens and back again daily. Yes, yes, yes.

* * *

Hold up, they don't love you like I love you.[34] The fall before "Formation" dropped, news about a black transwoman broke that you might have missed—but that I held onto like a gris-gris bag. In Minneapolis, transgender and anti-prison activist CeCe McDonald debuted electric turquoise braids swept into an elegant updo. Her followers raved, "Oh dear lard yes you are a sea foam goddess!" and "#SAYDAT #DON'T PLAYDAT Follow the movement!"[35] I have a huge, unapologetic girl crush on CeCe, the most intelligent person I've ever met and a staunch, intersectional activist for black women's rights who speaks and writes tirelessly about prison labor, women's reproductive rights, domestic violence, disability rights, and transmisogyny. And she's a sister Beyoncé fan of the highest order. "Beyoncé was *everything* to us," she shared at the talk she gave at UT Austin's "Afro Imaginative Symposium" in 2015, recalling her time living on the streets with black trans* sisters in Chicago.[36] When CeCe was released from a men's penitentiary after serving seventeen months for self-defense in January 2014, Laverne Cox was on hand with a limousine to escort her home. The two celebrated her hard-won release by enjoying the thing that CeCe had most missed while in prison: Beyoncé's self-titled visual album, which the women watched together on the drive.

The week before she debuted seafoam braids, CeCe championed fundraising for the funeral of slain college student and black transwoman Kiesha Jenkins and an investigation into her death, while her interview on Huffington Post went viral. So don't take it lightly if in the midst of all that, she got her hair done up like a sea goddess and posted about it. Every person who viewed and commented on her fine-ass photo was declaring *yes*, black transwomen have the divine right to be creative and joyful with their bodies and lives. Shouldn't black transwomen celebrate being on fleek, being in their brown skin and black hair looking good? And celebrate being sea foam goddesses, women with powers to make their own lives and looks shiny in a transmisogynoir climate that wants to bury them? *Slow down, they don't love you like I love you.*[37]

* * *

"'You got pretty hair,' Jamie said, staring at my wet curls with red-tinted eyes, 'Can I touch it?'" Janet Mock remembers her

1994 spring break crush asking. "I ducked underwater in re-sponse, swiftly swimming away from his compliment as my hair did its own floating, ethereal choreography in the blue that surrounded me."[38] Born in California and high schooled in Hawai'i, this black trans* journalist and activist spent her tween years in a Dallas suburb surrounded by her father's black woman-centered family. There—while presenting as a boy in school—afternoons and weekends she introduced her-self to friends as Keisha. "Keisha was more real to me than I was to myself," Janet explains. "She was fully me, the me I knew myself to be in those quiet instances when all I had to do was merely me."[39] While staying with her favorite Auntie Wee Wee and cousin Mechelle for spring break, Keisha found an ardent admirer in next door neighbor Jamie. And when he finally reached out to touch her hair, Keisha melted: "My hair, the only mark of my girlhood, was being touched in a way I had never been before."[40]

Like Laverne, Janet's femininity was visible to those around her early in life and gained her entry into her grandmother's Texas kitchen on Sunday afternoons while the Mock women made dinner. "*This is womanhood*, I thought, watching the women in Dad's life cook and cackle in the kitchen," she remembers.[41] From the Dallas Mocks, Janet learned black womanness is about intersectionality: "My grandmother and my two aunts were an exhibition in resilience and resource-fulness and black womanhood. They rarely talked about the unfairness of the world with the words that I use now with my social justice friends, words like *intersectionality* and *equality*, *oppression*, and *discrimination*. They didn't discuss those things because they were too busy living it, navigating it, surviving that."[42] She also learned that black womanhood is about treat-ing yourself as a work of art, announcing who you are with hair, clothes, and swag: like hairstylist Auntie Linda Gail's "long, honey-weave bang that sat prettily over her left eye," or

Auntie Wee Wee's lips "perpetually painted plum."[43] Political astuteness, self-determination, and self-aestheticizing go together in her formative family experiences of black womanhood, and their easy interflow shapes her feminism. "They were pleasure-seeking, resourceful, sexy, rhythmic, nurturing, fly, happy, stylish, rambunctious, gossipy, feeling, hurt, unapologetic women. They were the kind of women I wanted to be."[44]

Beyoncé was also one of Janet's black womanly ideals, from the moment she saw the MTV premiere of Destiny's Child's "Bills, Bills, Bills" and "was in awe of one girl, waving a hot comb in the air at her mother's Houston, Texas salon while lip-synching."[45] And like the rest of the Bey Hive, Janet was overjoyed by *Lemonade*'s release. "I think the evolution of Beyoncé, going from the girl power, to a feminist, to black power, and centering black womanhood is so vital . . . I think I see and read Beyoncé more in a peer lens. I've grown up with her," she confessed in an interview.[46] When Janet's friend, the black feminist theorist bell hooks, harshly critiqued *Lemonade* as an "utterly-aestheticized" vision of black womanhood and a "fashion plate fantasy,"[47] Janet clapped back with a response that shines with Auntie Linda Gail and Auntie Wee Wee's influence. "Femme feminists/writers/thinkers/artists are consistently dismissed, pressured to transcend presentation in order to prove our woke-ability. Our 'dressed up' bodies and 'big hair' do not make us any less serious," she tweeted. Janet fought her father, teachers, and colleagues for the right to grow her hair and let it down, and she'll fight for Beyoncé, too. "Femininity in general is seen as frivolous. People often say feminine people are doing 'the most,' meaning that to don a dress, heels, lipstick, and big hair is artifice, fake, and a distraction. But I knew even as a teenager that my femininity was more than just adornments: they were extensions of *me*, enabling me to express myself and my identity. My body, my clothes, and my makeup are on purpose, just as I am on purpose."[48] Big-hair Texas girls gotta stick together, too.

* * *

"Formation" opens with Beyoncé alone on top of a sinking police car, surrounded by floodwaters and singing the song's refrain: "Y'all haters corny with that Illuminati mess / Paparazzi, catch my fly and my funky fresh . . ."[49] But after Freedia's interlude the song starts over—the same way, but different. The scene cuts from the beauty shop to a line of black women in Gucci athletic wear seated at the bottom of a drained pool—water nowhere when it should be everywhere, instead of the opening flood of water everywhere when it should be nowhere—and the refrain begins again, this time over visuals of a legion of black women. The drained pool reflects historical realities in the post–civil rights South, where city after city drained public pools rather than allow blacks and whites to swim together. New Orleans closed its pools immediately after the passage of the 1964 Civil Rights Act and concerned citizen Cecil W. Carter confronted the mayor in 1965: "A year or so ago the public pools were drained under the pretext that the city of New Orleans lacked the funds to keep them open. Everybody knows, of course, that they were closed to avoid integration."[50] But this pool where black women *are* the water also concludes *Lemonade* by reworking metaphors of water and/as black womanness that run throughout the film. Water represents the contradictory, simultaneously oppressive and lifesaving possibilities of black femininity for the main character: "Hold Up" iconically begins with her floating underwater, drowning in betrayed black wifeness— then cuts to her in Oshun yellow cascading on a wave of water, newfound power in righteous black woman's anger buoying her up. In *Lemonade*'s earlier tracks, water-as-womanness is an external element the main character muscles though to find physical and emotional safety. But in this triumphant finale black women don't have to navigate water because they *are* water, their fluid movement filling an entire pool; they don't have to wrestle with the contradictory possibilities of black womanness as an outside force because they *are* black womanhood, a legion of sisters in formation.

Seated motionless on the pool floor in the first shot, the water-women return wielding curved hips and power fists to dance into a Malcolm-honoring X formation as the voiceover celebrates their woke-up-like-this flawlessness: "I love my baby hair with baby hair and Afros."[51] This time, because Big Freedia's interlude has intervened, the refrain can move into a chorus that triumphantly conjugates the verb Freedia introduced: "Cause I slay (slay), I slay (hey), I slay (okay), I slay (okay) / All day (okay), I slay (okay), I slay (okay), I slay (okay) / We gon' slay (slay), gon' slay (okay), we slay (okay), I slay (okay)."[52] And the pool dancers' formation returns for this first chorus, as water-blue-clad women dance in an X in an empty outdoor parking lot. The movement from black women drowning to slaying is enabled by Freedia's intervention: her lines are what makes the chorus possible, and her declaration of black feminine slayage is what opens space for Beyoncé and her dancers to become an ocean in the parking lot. *How* the contact with Freedia's black transfemininity makes Beyoncé's feminist formation possible is never made explicit, leaving viewers to imagine this connection on our own. And as I watch and try to connect, I always wonder: are there any black trans* women dancing in the parking lot as Beyoncé declares "we slay"? None of the dancers have identified themselves as trans*, to my knowledge, and probably none are. But there *needs* to be a black transwoman dancing to "I slay" to make good on the promise of black trans*- and cis-feminine collaboration that Freedia's interlude makes. So this time, I'm going to imagine one of the dozen dancers flanking Beyoncé—one of the dancers representing Louisiana, a state where 39 percent of the trans* population is black—is a flawlessly passing trans* woman. And next time I'm counting on Queen Bee to give us a black woman power anthem with Freedia or Janet or CeCe or Laverne (when she's not shooting three projects) or any other out black transwoman dancing beside her, slaying all day.

* * *

It's time to listen, it's time to fight. You've read this far, you see this last chapter moving to a close, you've noticed some of the elements that played louder in the earlier mixtapes—my loving focus on Queen Bee, my weaving in of my own stories—have faded out. Yes, that was a choice I made as part of imagining black trans*- and cisfeminism flowing together. Little privilege as we have in other domains, sometimes black cis women need to step aside from the defining role we've had in feminism: because our stories have been central to black feminism for too long, and even black cisfeminists who want to be transinclusive can fail to make room for trans* sisters. A well-intentioned bell hooks declared to Janet Mock that *all* black women have always been trans*, explaining: "the moment 'Ain't I a Woman' had to be addressed by Sojourner Truth, the moment she had to bare her breasts to prove that she was the woman, was already a . . . trans moment. So that rather than seeing ourselves as outside blackness, as outside the dialogue of queerness and trans I think that we need to place ourselves as black females at the core of the dialogue."[53] But *was* the challenge to Sojourner Truth's womanness the same as the challenge to Laverne Cox's, and *do* black cisfemales need to be at the core of the dialogue about black queer and transfeminism? All African-descended women face challenges to our femininity, yes, but Julia Serano speaks truth: "My very different trans history has led me to having a very different perspective on femininity and femme identity than that held by many of my cis femme sisters."[54] So sometimes, black cisfeminists need to move away from dancing at the center of the X and fiercely hold space for trans* sisters to publicize their brilliant choreographies of gender and survival. *Now we're going to hold doors open for a while, we're going to be open for a while.*

* * *

"Southern Trans Resistance is Beautiful," Miami native, Los Angeles–based dancer/choreographer Adisa Gooding posted for International Trans Visibility Day 2016, broadcasting an image of black transfemme Micky Bradford voguing at the North Carolina's governor's mansion to protest anti-trans* bathroom bill HB2.[55] That spring, Adisa collaborated with sister black trans* artist Miss Shalae to codirect their own vision of beautiful trans* resistance: "Lemonade Served Bitter Sweet," an eleven-minute remake of *Lemonade* videos "Hold Up," "Freedom," "Sorry," and "6 Inch." "My inspiration," Adisa explains to *Dance Mogul* magazine, "came from one, me personally being inspired by Miss Shalae who has been a strong and loving voice to and for trans women from minority backgrounds and two, her passion and own inspiration to do this project which stemmed from a deep love for Beyoncé."[56] Self-proclaimed "#1 Beyoncé impersonator in the world" Miss Shalae originally envisioned a #TransLivesMatter version of "Formation" but realized when *Lemonade* dropped "she could make her own homage using far fewer people." "So," Miss Shalae recounts, "I reached out to my co-director Adisa Gooding, and she used her contacts and we created the 'Lemonade' project under Glass Wing Group . . . a nonprofit organization for trans women of color."[57] Shot in Los Angeles in a single day, their "Lemonade" was explicitly transfeminist: "I want more than anything to inspire trans women, especially young trans women . . . I wanted to show that we are human first, and we are talented and we are able to create just like the next person."[58]

"Lemonade Served Bitter Sweet" opens with a fade-in of Pacific waves crashing to shore as foam-colored letters announce "GLASS WING COLLECTIVE PRESENTS."[59] The rush of ocean water is the video's first music, the camera cutting to waves that break over volcanic rocks and then to Miss Shalae posed regally in a flowing yellow dress with surf splashing her from shoulders to feet. "Hold Up" begins to play with the crash of a huge wave that Miss Shalae, now thigh-deep in the Pacific, welcomes with arms raised skyward. The "Bitter Sweet" star slays her opening shot in a yellow dress that replicates Beyoncé's Oshun dress while managing to be even more revealing—the cheetah-print bra Bey wears under her Roberto Cavalli gown replaced with a glimpse of Miss Shalae's perfect nipples; and references the crash of water that ushers Beyoncé into "Hold Up" but does so by harnessing the power of the Pacific, with no special effects involved. Where Beyoncé followed her waterborne entrance by bouncing down an unidentified street laughing as she smashed car windows and fire hydrants, Miss Shalae emerges from the ocean to stroll down the streets of Venice, Los Angeles. She commences her window-smashing when another member of the Glass Wing Collective hands her a bat labeled "HOT SAUCE" as Beyoncé sings, "What's worse, looking jealous or crazy?" After Miss Shalae shatters a car window, the camera cuts to a medium close-up of this friend rocking daisy dukes and a red bikini top, who flings her hair and screams with delight.

From "Hold Up" to "Formation"—from bedrooms filled to the ceiling with water to New Orleans streets disappeared under flooding—*Lemonade* curates fantastically *not* naturally occurring images of water-as-black-womanness. The main character almost drowns in the waters of black femininity because, whether inundating the private space of bedrooms or the public space of streets, these waters have been channeled in directions where they don't serve the main character. But unnatural waters have no place in "Lemonade Served Bitter Sweet"—and, I imagine, not only because of lack of a special effects budget. The opening scene of "Bitter Sweet" wades into the Pacific to put the force of the world's largest ocean behind its main character's femininity, breaking hard against violent dismissals of transwomanhood as having no natural place in the world. Instead, "Bitter Sweet" foregrounds natural bodies of water as "the embodiment of trans orientation," to borrow Dora Silva Santana's words, and black transfemininity as movement "across and along the waters, the imposed limits of gender, the secular and the sacred, the expectations of our death."[60] While it would be easy to map these films' images of water as running in vastly different directions—threatening drowning for Beyoncé but buoying Miss Shalae up—we can also follow them down paths where they interbraid like a bayou. Channeled together, the waters of *Lemonade* and "Bitter Sweet" suggest the *natural* condition of black womanhood—and by that I mean, the condition in which black women experience ourselves as *a force of nature*—has nothing to do with being cis or trans*. It has to do with standing in our power, stepping into to a vision of femininity we create in our own image, becoming the water in our empty pools or the force of the ocean at our back.

Adisa, Miss Shalae, and the Glass Wing Collective continue to create literally and figuratively moving images of black transfemininity. On March 16, 2017, they released a second video set to Jazmine Sullivan's "Mona Lisa" that features Miss Shalae mourning in a graveyard whose tombstones bear names of black transwomen killed in 2016 and 2017.[61] One of Miss Shalae's looks in this video—a crown of roses and spikes adorning long, wavy hair in a black-and-white close-up— echoes images from the pregnancy photoshoot Beyoncé posted the month before on Instagram, where she posed in a similar Virgin of Guadalupe–inspired crown captured in black and white. (Miss Shalae shared her enthusiasm for this shot when it circulated, posting it to her Instagram with the caption: "This is my favorite! Congrats Bey! Looking forward to the shower!"[62]) Both images of rose-crowned beauties artistically render black women *giving life*. Like "slay," "giving life" is a slang phrase that originated in black LGBT ball culture and crossed over to mainstream use (in large part through *RuPaul's Drag Race*). "Previous uses of 'give life' were mostly limited to 'mother' and 'God,'" Azizi Powell notes. "However, the vernacular saying can refer to . . . literally anything that gives an individual or group of people energy (vitality), validity, or significance."[63] And while the photoshoot of Beyoncé celebrates her literally giving life to twins, Adisa and Miss Shalae's video figuratively gives life to the black trans* women whose beauty they honor. "Dear world, stop killing us," the opening screen demands, then affirms: "Dear sisters, you are beautiful works of art, 'a masterpiece.'" When the Glass Wing Collective's videos went viral, Adisa and Miss Shalae sat for a flurry of interviews where they're inevitably asked if Beyoncé saw their loving homages. They don't know, Miss Shalae answers, "but she would 'love for her to' and hopes it will prompt her to join forces with Miss Shalae to 'eliminate the hate between cisgender women and trans-women.'"[64] *We gon' slay (slay), gon' slay (okay), we slay (okay), Beyoncé with Miss Shalae.*

* * *

The month after I wrote this chapter, five-hundred-year Atlantic Hurricane Harvey catastrophically flooded Beyoncé's native Houston, pouring a year's worth of rain onto the Bayou City in a seventy-two-hour period. On September 11, 2017, Beyoncé, Mama Tina, and Blue Ivy traveled together to meet with the city's displaced and distribute meals at her childhood church, St. John's United Methodist. Among the populations most disproportionately affected by the city's flooding are LGBT youth—especially black and Latina trans* women— who were at increased risk for homelessness before, during, and after the storm. "Houston officials did not order a mandatory evacuation before the storm that unleashed catastrophic flooding on the country's fourth largest city, which advocates say has become a refuge for lesbian, gay, bisexual, transgender and queer (LGBTQ) youth fleeing unaccepting homes throughout the South," NBC reporter Julie Compton notes.[65] One of these refugees is twenty-one-year-old Diva Richardson, who moved from New Orleans to Houston in May 2017 and found herself homeless when Harvey hit. "She wanted to be in a city that accepted her and where she could pursue her dream of being a singer," Compton notes. "She stayed briefly at a friend's home, she said, but left after they got into an argument. From there she went to a local homeless shelter, she said, where some of the residents verbally abused her."[66] At the time of this writing, Diva Richardson was staying in a Salvation Army Family Residence with a supportive male roommate. This chapter is dedicated to Diva and all the Gulf Coast's black trans* women, who need black feminist solidarity now more than ever. May Beyoncé's next visit to Houston be not to visit Diva at the Salvation Army Residence, but to hear her sing like a bird.

OUTRO
I KNOW BEYONCÉ LOVES BLACK FEMMES

"HAPPY BIRTHDAY BEYONCÉ FROM YOUR FAMILY AND FRIENDS" beyonce.com announced on September 4, 2017, its simple birthday wish signed by eighteen black-and-white portraits of the singer's nearest and dearest.[1] Michelle Obama, Serena Williams, Tina Knowles Lawson, Bianca Lawson, Kelly Rowland, and Halley and Chloe Bailey were among the black luminaries who posed in homage to "Formation," sporting wide-brimmed black hats, dramatic lipstick, long plaits, elaborate bib necklaces, and off-the-shoulder tops replicating Bey's iconic conjure woman swag. Blue Ivy's picture sits nestled under her mother's name at the top right corner, cradled below by an identically dressed image of her paternal grandmother Gloria Carter. The next day, Ms. Gloria was the featured guest on Tidal's D'USSÉ Friday podcast. There she discussed her collaboration with son Jay Z on *4:44*, released in June 2017 as an answer record to the *Lemonade* his wife poured the spring before. Ms. Gloria appears on the third and longest track, "Smile," where—after Jay reveals in the first verse that "Mama had four kids but she a lesbian / Had to pretend so long she's a thespian"[2]—she closes the song with a poem she wrote to "help him" tell her story.[3] "Living in the shadows. Can you imagine what kind of life it is to live? In the shadows people see you as happy and free. Because that's what you want them to see. Living two lives, happy but not free," she opens her outro, and leaves with the advice: "But life is short, and it's time to be free. Love who you love, because life isn't guaranteed. Smile."[4] On the podcast, Ms. Gloria confirmed her love of women has *never* been a secret from her family and friends: why would it be? "I was never ashamed of me . . . Everybody knows who I am. I don't hide who I am," she declares with the inimitable dignity of a black grandmother. "I don't have to worry about nobody wondering whether I'm in the life or not. I'm gonna tell 'em. So now that I told you, what do you have to talk about?"[5]

When "Smile" dropped two weeks after the birth of Carter twins Rumi and Sir, queer folk everywhere had Ms. Gloria to talk about. Austin-based, nonbinary black lesbian blogger Alaina Monts marveled on queer women's blog Autostraddle: "Beyoncé's husband released a new album, but what I'm excited about is the track titled 'Smile' where his mother, Gloria Carter, comes out as a lesbian."[6] GLAAD president Sarah Kate Ellis issued this statement: "Lesbian women are all too often erased or excluded from narratives surrounding LGBTQ people. By sharing her truth with the world, Gloria Carter is increasing visibility of lesbian women of color at a critical time and sending a powerful message of empowerment to the entire LGBTQ community that is perfectly timed with the end of Pride Month."[7] Black trans* journalist Tiq Milan— whose brilliant black femme activist-writer wife, Kim Katrin Milan, shares my birthday—told *Billboard* he was "pleasantly surprised that [JAY Z] invited us into that part of his life. My wife and I were sitting there listening to it and we both got teary eyed."[8] And of course I was talking about Ms. Gloria, too, whose "Smile" changed how I look at Beyoncé's family. When the first paparazzi photos of the twins surfaced—Mama Bey holding Sir while Grandma Gloria cradled Rumi on vacation in Miami—I thought, *Beyoncé's daughter is being loved into this world by a black lesbian.* When Ms. Gloria posed in wig, lipstick, and statement necklace for Beyoncé's birthday gallery, I saw: *a black lesbian is sending a message of love in formation with Beyoncé.*

When Ms. Gloria came out, I rushed to search engines with the burning hope that maybe, just maybe—like so many women who marry men and have children before entering "in the life" (as Ms. Gloria calls it)—Beyoncé's children's grandmother is a black femme, too. But Google news and image searches told a different story. Photographing her in locs, camouflage hoodies, and suit jackets, gossip blogs labeled Ms. Gloria a "butch"[9] who was currently "booed up"[10] with "PYT,"[11] "Latina Lipstick Lesbian"[12] Dania Diaz. No online bios surface for Dania, who works as executive director of the Shawn Carter Scholarship Foundation alongside Ms. Gloria and shows up in photos with loosely waved, long hair and bright lipstick. So I did what any Piscean practitioner of black femme magic would do: I made up her backstory. Yes, I imagined a black queer fairy tale starring Dania as a Dominican York femme who lets Ms. Gloria open doors for her as she walks by in six-inch heels, vibes on Cardi B, Whitney Houston, and Diana Ross, wears La Perla lingerie to Brooklyn Black Pride and anti-Trump protests. A black power femme who sometimes talks with daughter-in-law Beyoncé about what it's like to be the younger wife of a Carter, about being in the same industry as your partner but getting less respect than your masculine boo, about which of Grandma Hattie's recipes is the best and who made a fool of themselves at the last family event. In my fairy tale, Beyoncé loves a black femme as one of her own.

This book has been a love letter from one black femme to Beyoncé. And as I was finishing it and dreaming of Bey's daughterly intimacies with the Dania of my imagination, I realized: I don't want to end without opening space to fabulate some of the many ways Beyoncé might return black femmes' love. So I asked some beautiful, brilliant young black queers in my life to imagine: if you got to meet Beyoncé, what would it be like? How would she show her love for you? My first answer came from the amazing Candice Lyons, the best research assistant in the history of black queer academia, who took time out from contemplating the many PhD programs she was accepted into to spin this short and perfect tale: "In my dream meeting with Beyoncé, she would first find a way to casually confirm my deep-seated belief that she's a solid two on the Kinsey Scale (at the very least). Then, she'd tell me she likes my lipstick and offer to take a selfie."[13] Will Mosley, a PhD student writing a laser-sharp dissertation on black queer expressive culture in the US South while podcasting in his free time, surprised me with a thoroughly Texan fantasy: "My dream meeting with Beyoncé would take place at the Texas State Fair. We'd split an elephant ear, ride the Ferris wheel, and she'd teach me how to line dance (elephant emoji, Ferris wheel emoji, two girls dancing emoji)."[14] And he explained: "As a graduate student in my late twenties, my adult life can be divided into two phases, pre– and post–*Self Titled*. Life in the wake of Beyoncé is impromptu dance parties, celebrating the milestones of my QTPOC chosen family, and them loving me back. Everything before this is just preamble."[15]

Dr. Jacqueline Smith, certified yoga teacher and poet, took a minute in the midst of her work for reproductive justice for black women in Texas to dream across generations:

> Our day will consist of a brunchtime fest with a group of my most cherished Black women fam, friends and allies, surrounded by sun-kissed flowers, warm lighting, and in-person serenades from Etta James, Nina Simone, Sade, Tina Turner, Chaka Khan, just to name a few. With frosted, chilled glasses of lemonade, and generous portions of honey-drizzled fried chicken, cornbread, and greens, we will talk and laugh, sing and play while we make Black Girl majic!!!! The luncheon will conclude with lemon-frosted cupcakes and attendees' karaoke style tribute to Bey. Dancing is suggested, but not required.

Following rest, naps, and spa treatments, me and the beehive massive will end our evening under spectacular lights and bling, with front row, VIP tickets to an exclusive concert by Queen Bey!! Me and my crew will sing, dance, and laugh with and for ourselves, as we celebrate Beyoncé, Black Femme/Woman KNOWING, DREAMING, and THRIVING!!! And, of course, there will be a twerk or 2 . . . while we join N Formation. Who Runs the World? Black Girls!!![16]

But no one outdid standout 2018 Beyoncé Feminism student, African and African diaspora studies major, and fashion icon Jarvis Dillard, who identified himself the first day of class as the world's biggest Beyoncé stan and sang and danced along to "Mi Gente" in the packed lecture hall to prove it. Jarvis imagined *three* dream meetings with Beyoncé, each where Queen Bey serendipitously appears to give him exactly the kind of love he needs at that moment of his life. His brilliance:

Being the biggest Beyoncé fan, which I've titled myself, I've thought long and hard about what I would do and say when I finally got the opportunity to meet Beyoncé. Beyoncé gave me so much confidence as a young gay child to be as feminine as I wanted to be and to take notes. I was Sasha Fierce, but in private. If I were to meet her at that age, I would've wanted to put on some heels and a wig and to show her herself in me. I perfected every step, ad-lib and hair flip that made her the powerful performer she has become and feel that she would've greatly appreciated the time I spent learning her moves and perfecting her persona. In my head, she was the female version of me. As I grew up, she grew up with me. We both experienced more, learned more, figured out who we were as people. Because I don't know her personally, we only interact with each other through her music and I felt her passion and devotion and drive and skill on every song and on every level; from the viewpoint I have as a man and the viewpoint I most relate to, which is that of a woman.

A couple of years later she released her self-titled album that to me solidified her spot as an ICON. An unpublicized visual album that stopped the world, is how I would describe it. It showed her fans a side to her that we had never seen before: her openness to be unorthodox and be a powerful sexual character while still being super feminine. If I met her around this time, I would still want to dance for her but I'd ask so many questions. Where do your ideas come from? Why are you so legendary? How do you think you've inspired millions of your fans that have watched you grow up with them? The questions would go on as long as they could and as long as they would let me. She's from Houston, like myself, and I can't think of a better person that could encourage a black gay male to believe in the power that he has within to reach goals never reached before.

Fast-forward to February 7, 2016. I'm in college now, and with the Super Bowl falling on my birthday, my god-brother playing in the game and Beyoncé set to perform at halftime, I believed it would be a great day. I remember saying in the days leading up to the game, "Beyoncé should give me something for my birthday!" And who would have known that the day before, she would drop an anthem for all black women to bathe in their melanin glory for years to come? People say they'll always remember where they were when 9/11 happened and when JFK's assassination occurred. I specifically remember what I was doing when *Lemonade* dropped.

Without knowing much about the samples she used and references she was making, I felt that she was showing her true and raw blackness that would cause the music industry to stop and take notice. In this era and the most recent times in our life, I would want to sit down and first take in the woman whose name itself is worth millions of dollars. I would then want to know not who the stage Beyoncé is or the things we all know about her, but the things not many people know. She always has her guard up in every situation but I would want for her to break down that wall and talk to me how she would with Jay, Blue, Tina and Solange. For her to sit with me like one of the girls and just talk.[17]

Fabulous. Ten years ago, my soft-spoken, brilliant black butch colleague Kara Keeling invented a name for the kind of imaginative play I asked these young black queers to indulge in and that they took to the next level. *The black femme function*, she calls it. Because characters who are ultra feminine, decidedly queer, and unapologetically black *at the same time* so rarely appear on screen, Kara muses, when one does, she offers "a reminder that the set of what appears is never perfectly closed and that something different might appear therein at any-instant-whatever."[18] She opens a slim space to imagine that different configurations of gender, race, and sexuality—one where all the women aren't white, all the blacks aren't men, and all the queers aren't butch—can exist and flourish in the misogynoir, femmephobic, homophobic world we navigate. In that way, Kara writes, black femme characters become "a portal to a reality that does not operate according to" the rules of dominant culture.[19] Now, *Lemonade*-era Beyoncé is ultra feminine and unapologetically black, yes, but not queer—she hasn't confirmed she's at least a two on the Kinsey scale *yet*. But in the absence of out black queer femme media figures who reflect us, femme-leaning and -loving black queer folk claim Beyoncé's black-woman-loving spectacularness as our portal to alternative realities where "Who Runs the World? Black Girls!!!" A portal to realities where the past lovingly meets the present, where Nina Simone and Etta James sit down with us for Sunday brunch; where the Texas present celebrates black queers, dancing us through the state fair; where the future is an open field of possibilities and "a black gay male [can] believe in the power that he has within to reach goals never reached before." A portal to a world where our cultural landmarks aren't histories of violence—9/11 and the Kennedy assassination—but the hard blossoming of black women's creativity, gifting *Lemonade* to our queer springs.

Over Thanksgiving break 2018, Baía and I planned a trip we hoped would open its own kind of portal. Bee and I love going to Louisiana any time, for any reason; Many, Pleasant Hill, Lake Charles, Baton Rouge, New Orleans, wherever we go we feel at home. Mary Davis, Mary Davis, Mary Davis, your great-granddaughters love coming home. So while Matt refused to come with us—you *know* that place is haunted, he insisted—Baía and I joyfully flew and drove to spend two days at Madewood Plantation in Napoleonville, Louisiana, where Beyoncé filmed *Lemonade*. We stayed in the nursery where "Daddy Lessons" was filmed and Baía enjoyed mothering an antique baby doll while pretending to be a young plantation mistress who ran the white folk out, freed the slaves, and became a single mother. Of course, I took endless pictures of her: with the baby doll, in the formal dining room where she was served a three-course dinner by white folk, on the balcony, with the plantation's black cat, flipping back handsprings across the front lawn cleared by slaves. And I took shot after shot of Baía smiling as wide as June sprawled out over the chair where Serena twerked for Beyoncé. I asked innkeeper Angie, who took impeccable care of us during our too-short

Baía at Madewood Plantation.

stay, whether many *Lemonade*-inspired tourists came through and she confirmed that they did, inevitably taking pictures on the "Sorry" throne. How many black Southern lesbians sat our luxurious asses on that throne, I wondered, feeling jubilant that Beyoncé and Serena cleared this plantation space for us to enjoy the love black women carry for each other? How many swung on the swing Beyoncé's team hung in the back yard? How many made love in the master bedroom, negotiating who's going to roleplay Queen Bee this time—"Come sit on mama lap, hey!"?[20]

Mother dearest, let us inherit *this* earth. As we left, Baía and I made a promise to ourselves to come back to Madewood once a year—this year, I hope, for my birthday weekend. Will I have family and friends take pictures in "Sorry"-themed outfits and post them under the heading "HAPPY BIRTHDAY OMI FROM YOUR FAMILY AND FRIENDS?" Probably not. Our plan to return to Madewood isn't an act of reverence for Beyoncé, really. Marking her healthy differentiation from her mother, Baía has made clear she's no longer a Beyoncé fan—she's still there for Blue Ivy, though. Our annual pilgrimage would be an act of reverence *for ourselves*: for our black womanness, our Louisiananaess, our sorry not sorryness, our baby hair Afro yellow bone-ness, our black mamadaughter love, our black femme magic. This is the Beyoncé feminism I want to pass on to my daughter: when life serves you *Lemonade*, celebrate yourself.

ACKNOWLEDGMENTS

First, thanks to my editor at University of Texas Press, Casey Kittrell. When he sent a kind email inquiring whether I'd be interested in writing a book on Beyoncé, he opened the door to realize a dream I didn't even know I had. Then he made himself available to talk through every idea, draft, and possible title, even offering to bring me soup when I was working through the flu. Huge thanks as well to the outside reviewers of this text, especially the brilliant Kinitra Brooks, my sister Beyoncé feminist scholar-warrior at the University of Texas at San Antonio, who read the text and offered commentary as beautiful and generous as her own scholarship.

This book grew out of a class I've had the privilege to teach titled Beyoncé Feminism, Rihanna Womanism. And it never would have come into being without all my wonderful colleagues who supported this course when I came up with the crazy idea for it. Jackie Salcedo, Nia Crosley, Kali N. Gross, Ted Gordon, Sue Heinzelman, and Kevin Foster, thank you for publicizing the class, trying to reach Beyoncé on Instagram, finding the best and brightest lecture rooms, trying to offer Beyoncé an honorary degree, chasing the dream of a Beyoncé Knowles-Carter Endowed Chair, and letting me share Beyoncé Feminism on the award-winning television series *Blackademics*. Of course, eternal gratitude goes to the most dedicated student in the history of the Beyoncé class, Miss Robin Moten, who delayed graduation a semester to take the course and has become an amazing support, friend, and godmother to my child in the years since.

I had the good fortune of working with the best research assistant in the history of black queer academia, Candice Lyons, whose thoughtful commentary shaped the text in ways seen and unseen throughout. Jacqueline Smith, Karly Randolph Pitman, Helen Tinsley-Jones, Nicole Ofstad, and Matt Richardson were also kind enough to read early drafts of proposals and chapters and to offer their input. Thank you so very much for giving me the chance to connect with you through this work.

A deep, heartfelt bow-down to all my colleagues who supported me through the difficult times I faced while writing this. At the University of Texas at Austin, Karma Chavez, Liz Cullingford, Ann Cvetkovich, Nancy Ewert, Brian Evans, Alan Friedman, Lyndon Gill, Ted Gordon, Laura Gutierrez, Sue Heinzelman, Pat Heisler, Omi Osun Jones, Xavier Livermon, Lisa C. Moore, Roger Reeves, Sharmila Rudrappa, Jackie Salcedo, and Christen Smith: always in formation. My yoga teachers and colleagues, Mary Richardson, Kewal Hausmann, Shelby Autrey, Mike Matsumura, and Christine Rodriguez, who kept me sane and strong. And to my nationwide queer/feminist scholar squadron: Jafari Allen, Marlon Bailey, Ananya Chatterjea, Jigna Desai, Lisa Duggan, Cindy Garcia, Jack Halberstam, Marcia Ochoa, Annelise Orleck, Juliana Hu Pegues, Juana Rodriguez, C. Riley Snorton, and Lamonda Horton Stallings, who gave me hope for a queer future.

While I was writing this, I received several kind invitations to lecture about my work on Beyoncé. Thank you to the Center for the Study of Women at UCLA for inviting me to give the keynote lecture at the 2017 Thinking Gender Conference, and to the Department of English at Emory University for bringing me in as the 2017 Kemp Malone lecturer. Most especial thanks to Kinitra Brooks and Kameelah Martin for organizing an amazing Feminist Research Seminar at the University of Michigan's Institute for Research on Women and Gender, "Beyoncé's Lemonade Lexicon: Black Feminism and Spirituality in Theory & Praxis." There, for three magical days in the Ann Arbor fall, I shared black feminist critical perspectives and life-changing experiences with Kinitra, Kameelah, Candice Benbow, Regina Bradley, Tanisha Ford, Janell Hobson, Birgitta Johnson, Nicholas Jones, LaKisha Simmons, and Lindsey Stewart. The symposium was magical, inspirational, and paradigm-shifting.

This book is the story of my friends and family, too, who generously shared memories and thoughts with me to pass on to readers. Thank you to my family: my grandmother, Herta Stapler; my mother, Helen Tinsley-Jones, and my father, Jim Tinsley; my sisters Nicole Ofstad and Christina Tinsley; my uncle Tony Tinsley and my cousin Laurel Tinsley. And to my friends, colleagues, and students, Corinne, Elizabeth, and Craig Hampton, Jacque Smith, Candice Lyons, Kimari Brand, Will Mosely, and Jarvis Dillard, for letting slivers of your lives become part of this book.

And to my beloved husband Matt, who's not a Beyoncé fan but has waded through endless hours of conversation about her, who guards his privacy but let me make him a character in this book, who loves and supports me in every way and everything that makes me happy. Yes, there's every reason "Halo" makes me think of you. Baía, baby girl, this book is for you in every way. You are my living, breathing, flying, back-handspringing, dancing reminder that a black feminist future in the US South is here, unstoppable, and beautiful. And last but not least, Dulce, Ashanti, Oji, Nunu, Zora, and August: you cuddled me when I needed it, and Beyoncé would want you all to have extra treats.

NOTES

INTRODUCTION

1. Beyoncé quoted by Victoria Dawson Hoff, "Beyonce Just Released a Very Personal Short Film on Feminism, Body Image, and Life," http://www.elle.com/culture/movies-tv/news/a19631/beyonce-yours -and-mine-video/. Accessed October 29, 2017.
2. Marlon M. Bailey, Priya Kandaswamy, and Mattie Udora Richard-son, "Is Gay Marriage Racist?" in *That's Revolting! Queer Strategies for Resisting Assimilation*, ed. Mattilda, AKA Matt, Bernstein Syca-more (Brooklyn: Soft Skull Press, 2004), 92.
3. See this promo at https://www.youtube.com/watch?v= d8J3uQpLiUM. Accessed October 29, 2017.
4. Terryn Hall, "Southern Girl: Beyoncé, Badu, and Southern Black Womanhood," http://therumpus.net/2016/06/southern-girl -Beyoncé-badu-and-southern-black-womanhood/. Accessed De-cember 6, 2016.
5. Sydney Gore, "'Lemonade': A Love Letter From Beyoncé to Black Women," http://www.nylon.com/articles/Beyoncé-lemonade-review. Accessed December 6, 2016.
6. Hall, "Southern Girl."
7. For a summary of these debates, see Janell Hobson, "Feminists Debate Beyoncé," in *The Beyoncé Effect: Essays on Sexuality, Race, and Feminism*, ed. Adrienne Trier-Bienieck (Jefferson, NC: McFar-land & Company, 2016). One of the most trenchant and important objections to Beyoncé's feminism is the criticism that Beyoncé's participation in capitalism is antifeminist. While Beyoncé's failure to critique capitalism is a difference between her feminist politics and mine, I do not think that it disqualifies her as a feminist.
8. Janet Mock, "How Beyoncé Pushed Me to Call Myself a Feminist," https://janetmock.com/2014/09/03/beyonce-feminist-mtv-vmas/. Ac-cessed October 29, 2017.
9. See Jessica Bennett, "How to Reclaim the F-Word? Just Call Beyoncé," http://time.com/3181644/beyonce-reclaim-feminism-pop-star/. Accessed October 29, 2017.
10. Hobson, "Feminists Debate," 24.
11. Sublimefemme, https://sublimefemme.wordpress.com/2008/10/27 /rethinking-high-femme-part-1/. Accessed December 6, 2016.

12. Sydney Fonteyn Lewis, "'Everything I Know About Being a Black Femme I Learned from *Sula*': Or, Towards a Black Femme-inist Criticism." *Trans-scripts* 2 (2012), 105.
13. Laini Madhubuti, "Femme Invisibility," in *Naked: Black Women Bare All about Their Skin, Hair, Hips, Lips, and Other Parts*, ed. Ayana D. Byrd and Akiba Solomon (New York: Berkley Publishing, 2005), 141.
14. Ozy Frantz, "Femmephobia: 'Girls Are Gross' Writ Large," https://goodmenproject.com/featured-content/femmephobia-girls-are-gross-writ-large/. Accessed October 29, 2017.
15. Annie Lennox quoted by Chris Azzopardi, "Annie Lennox on Her Legacy, Why Beyonce Is 'Feminist Lite,'" http://www.pridesource.com/article.html?article=68228. Accessed October 29, 2017.
16. Hobson, "Feminists Debate," 17.
17. Kaila Adia Story, "Fear of a Black Femme: The Existential Co-nundrum of Embodying a Black Femme Identity while Being a Professor of Black, Queer, and Feminist Studies," *Journal of Lesbian Studies* 21:4 (2017), 410.
18. S. Lewis, "'Everything I Know,'" 118.
19. S. Lewis, "'Everything I Know,'" 101.
20. S. Lewis, "'Everything I Know,'" 101.
21. S. Lewis, "'Everything I Know,'" 122.
22. Evelyn Ngugi, "Call in Black," https://www.youtube.com/watch?v=cpVeUVcFMAU. Accessed February 16, 2017.
23. Heather Love, "Truth and Consequences: On Paranoid Reading and Reparative Reading," *Criticism* 52:2 (Spring 2010), 235.
24. Eve Sedgwick, *Touching Feeling: Affect, Pedagogy, Performativity* (Durham, NC: Duke University Press, 2002).
25. Femme on a Mission, "10 Famous Femme Lesbians on Coming Out," https://femmeonamission.com/2011/07/28/10-famous-femme-lesbians-on-coming-out/. Accessed October 29, 2017.
26. Del Lagrace Volcano and Ulrike Dahl, *Femmes of Power: Exploding Queer Femininities* (London: The Serpent's Tail, 2008), 26.
27. S. Lewis, "'Everything I Know,'" 101.
28. Ann Cvetkovich, *An Archive of Feelings* (Durham, NC: Duke University Press, 2003), 165.
29. Juana Maria Rodriguez, *Sexual Futures, Queer Gestures, and Other Latina Longings* (New York: New York University Press, 2014), 17.
30. Tamara Palmer, *Country Fried Soul: Adventures in Dirty South Hip Hop* (San Francisco: Backbeat Press, 2005), 10.
31. Palmer, *Country Fried Soul*, 13.

32. American Studies Association, https://www.theasa.net/annual-meeting/years-meeting/dissent-mixtape. Accessed October 29, 2017.

QUEEN BEE BLUES

1. See Daniel Kreps's discussion of the *Lemonade* announcement in *Rolling Stone*, "Beyoncé Teases 'World Premiere Event' for 'Lemonade,'" http://www.rollingstone.com/music/news/beyonce-tease-world-premiere-event-for-lemonade-20160416. Accessed March 15, 2017.

2. See the *Lemonade* trailer at https://www.youtube.com/watch?v=BB5zLq1zcdo. Accessed March 15, 2017. Transcription mine.

3. *Lemonade* is available on the Tidal streaming service at https://listen.tidal.com/video/59727844. Accessed March 15, 2017.

4. Quoted by Jessie Dean Altman in "Confused Beyoncé Fans Are Going after Rachel Ray Instead of Rachel Roy," http://www.someecards.com/entertainment/celebrities/beyonce-fans-confused-rachael-ray-rachel-roy/. Accessed March 15, 2017.

5. Cultured Creole, "Is *Lemonade* Beyoncé's Confessions?" https://www.culturedcreole.com/blog/2016/4/25/is-lemonade-beyonces-confessions. Accessed March 15, 2017.

6. Quoted by Meg Kehoe, "Is Beyonce's 'Lemonade' about Divorce? Twitter Seems to Think So," https://www.romper.com/p/is-beyonces-lemonade-about-divorce-twitter-seems-to-think-so-9437. Accessed March 15, 2017.

7. Lowkey Jenni quoted by Mustafa Gatollari in "25 Tweets About Jay-Z Getting Destroyed by Lemonade That Are Just Too Real," http://distractify.com/humor/2016/04/26/jay-z-lemonade. Accessed March 15, 2017.

8. Quoted by Orli Matlow in "The 32 Best Twitter Reactions to 'Lemonade,' Beyoncé's Sweet and Sour Masterpiece," http://www.someecards.com/entertainment/music/beyonce-jay-z-twitter-reactions/. Accessed March 15, 2017.

9. Angela Davis, *Blues Legacies and Black Feminism: Gertrude 'Ma' Rainey, Bessie Smith, and Billie Holiday* (New York: Vintage, 1999), 18, 20.

10. See "Crazy in Love" at https://www.youtube.com/watch?v=ViwtNLUqkMY. Accessed March 15, 2017.

11. Transcription of "Don't Hurt Yourself" lyrics taken from Lyrics Genius: https://genius.com/Beyonce-dont-hurt-yourself-lyrics. Accessed March 15, 2017.

12. Quoted on Wikipedia, "Crazy in Love," https://en.wikipedia.org

/wiki/Crazy_in_Love#cite_ref-105. Accessed March 15, 2017.

13. I listened to "Birmingham Blues" and transcribed the lyrics from the recording at https://www.youtube.com/watch?v=VVcEFZlyl1Y. Accessed March 15, 2017.

14. See Black German Cultural Society, "Germany's Brown Babies," http://afrogermans.us/german-brown-babies-2/. Accessed March 15, 2017.

15. This magazine cover is reproduced on the Black German Cultural Society website.

16. Beyoncé, "Hold Up" lyrics transcribed on Lyrics Genius, https://genius.com/Beyonce-hold-up-lyrics. Accessed March 15, 2017.

17. James Cone, *The Spirituals and the Blues* (Maryknoll, New York: Orbis Books, 1991 [1971]), 104.

18. Candice Lyon, personal communication, March 10, 2017.

19. Lyrics transcribed by Davis in *Blues Legacies*, 200.

20. Davis, *Blues Legacies*, 22.

21. Transcribed by Davis in *Blues Legacies*, 238.

22. Paul and Beth Garon, *Woman with Guitar: Memphis Minnie's Blues* (San Francisco: City Lights, 2014), 219–220.

23. Transcribed by Davis in *Blues Legacies*, 287.

24. Davis, *Blues Legacies*, 37.

25. See Beyoncé's video "Why Don't You Love Me?" at https://www.youtube.com/watch?v=QczgvUDskk0. Accessed March 16, 2017.

26. Davis, *Blues Legacies*, 21.

27. Quoted in Garon and Garon, *Woman with Guitar*, 90.

28. Quoted in Garon and Garon, *Woman with Guitar*, 178.

29. Quoted in Garon and Garon, *Woman with Guitar*, 89, 90.

30. Quoted by Garon and Garon, *Woman with Guitar*, 38.

31. See Jas Obrecht, *Early Blues: The First Stars of Blues Guitar* (Minneapolis: University of Minnesota Press, 2015).

32. Paul Garon, "Memphis Minnie," in *Encyclopedia of the Blues*, vol. 2, ed. Edward Komara (New York: Routledge, 2006), 687.

33. Quoted in Garon and Garon, *Woman with Guitar*, 159.

34. Quoted in Garon and Garon, *Woman with Guitar*, 49.

35. Garon and Garon, *Woman with Guitar*, 50.

36. Lyrics transcribed on SongLyrics, http://www.songlyrics.com/memphis-minnie/when-the-levee-breaks-lyrics/. Accessed March 16, 2017.

37. This speech can be viewed at https://www.youtube.com/watch?v=sCSOiN_38nE. Accessed March 16, 2016.

38. See Beth Richie's powerful *Arrested Justice: Black Women, Violence, and America's Prison Nation* (New York: New York University Press, 2012), 125–156.

39. Ebony Utley, "When Better Becomes Worse: Black Wives Describe Their Experiences with Infidelity," *Black Women, Gender, and Families* 5:1 (Spring 2011), 75.

40. Quoted in Utley, "When Better Becomes Worse," 76.

41. Hortense Spillers, "Mama's Baby, Papa's Maybe: An American Grammar Book," *Diacritics* 17:2 (Summer 1987), 80.

42. Quoted by Garon and Garon in *Woman with Guitar*, 174.

43. Davis, *Blues Legacies*, 106.

44. Garon and Garon, *Woman with Guitar*, 32.

45. Garon and Garon, *Woman with Guitar*, 32.

46. Quoted by Nick Hasted in *Jack White: How He Built an Empire from the Blues* (London: Omnibus Press, 2016).

47. Ray Suarez, "Jack White on Beyoncé, Detroit, and Where Songs Come From," http://www.npr.org/2016/09/10/493177019/jack -white-on-detroit-beyonc-and-where-songs-come-from. Accessed March 16, 2017.

48. Brittany Spanos, "How Beyoncé's 'Lemonade' Reclaims Rock's Black Female Legacy," http://www.rollingstone.com/music /news/how-beyonces-lemonade-reclaims-rocks-black-female -legacy-20160426. Accessed March 16, 2017.

49. Spanos, "How Beyoncé's 'Lemonade' Reclaims."

50. Candice Lyons, personal communication, March 10, 2017.

51. Quoted by Iona Kirby, "Beyoncé Hints at the Meaning behind Blue Ivy's Unusual Name with Telling Tumblr Post," http://www.daily mail.co.uk/tvshowbiz/article-2159507/Beyonc-hints-meaning-Blue -Ivys-unusual-telling-Tumblr-post.html. Accessed October 25, 2017.

52. See Koko Taylor's interview in *Blues Story: A Documentary*, https:// www.youtube.com/watch?v=5qq_qnLHf74. Accessed March 16, 2017.

MAMA SAID SHOOT

1. Spencer Kornhaber, "What Beyonce's 'Daddy Lessons' Had to Teach," https://www.theatlantic.com/entertainment/archive/2016/11 /cmas-beyonce-daddy-lessons-dixie-chicks-country-music-awards -race/506375/. Accessed October 25, 2017.

2. Quoted by Caitlin White, "The Internet Absolutely Loved Beyonce and The Dixie Chicks' Supergroup Performance of 'Daddy Lessons,'" http://uproxx.com/music/beyonce-cma-performance -reactions/. Accessed October 25, 2017.

3. Quoted by Joe Coscarelli, "Beyonce's C.M.A. Awards Performance Becomes the Target of Backlash," https://www.nytimes.

com/2016/11/04/arts/music/beyonce-cma-awards-backlash.html. Accessed October 25, 2017.

4. Quoted by Lauren Matthews, "Travis Tritt Went on an Epic Twitter Rant Over Beyonce's CMA Awards Performance," http://www.countryliving.com/life/entertainment/news/a40450/travis-tritt-beyonce-cma-performance/. Accessed October 25, 2017.

5. Quoted in "They Mad: People Aren't Happy Beyoncé is Performing at the CMAs," https://www.bet.com/music/2016/11/02/they-mad—people-aren-t-happy-beyonce-is-performing-at-the-cmas.html. Accessed October 27, 2017.

6. Andrea Grimes on Twitter, https://twitter.com/andreagrimes/status/725367189994242049. Accessed October 27, 2017.

7. Comment to "Beyonce shocks CMA awards," http://messwith yourhead.com/beyonce-shocks-cma-awards/. Accessed October 25, 2017.

8. Diane Pecknold and Kristine McCusker, "Introduction" to *Country Boys and Redneck Women: New Essays in Gender and Country Music* (Jackson: University Press of Mississippi, 2016), 13.

9. Alan Jackson, "Home" on *Here in the Real World* (Arista, 1990).

10. Chris Stapleton quoted by Nick Murray, "Chris Stapleton on Meeting Beyonce, Writing with Dwight Yoakam," http://www.rollingstone.com/country/news/chris-stapleton-on-meeting-beyonc-writing-with-yoakam-w448622. Accessed October 25, 2017.

11. Beth Richie, *Compelled to Crime: The Gender Entrapment of Black Women* (New York: Routledge, 1996), 40.

12. Richie, *Compelled to Crime*, 43.

13. Julia Brucculieri, "Dolly Parton's CMAs Speech Is Another Reason We'll Always Love Her," https://www.huffingtonpost.com/entry/dolly-parton-lifetime-achievement-award-cmas_us_581b2a3ae4b0c43e6c1e344d. Accessed October 25, 2017.

14. Quoted by Dave Paulson, "Dolly Parton's 'Touching' CMA Awards Tribute," http://www.tennessean.com/story/entertainment/music/2016/11/03/dolly-partons-touching-cma-awards-tribute/93223728/. Accessed October 25, 2017.

15. Dolly Parton, *Dolly: My Life And Other Unfinished Business* (New York: Harper Collins, 1994).

16. D. Parton, *Dolly*, 33.

17. Dolly Parton, "Mama" on *Pure & Simple* (Dolly Records, 2016).

18. Stella Parton, *Tell It Sister, Tell It: Memories, Music, and Miracles* (Attic Entertainment, 2011), 59.

19. S. Parton, *Tell It Sister*, 60.

20. Stella Parton, "Up in the Holler" on *Appalachian Blues* (Raptor Records, 2001).

21. D. Parton, *Dolly*, 58.

22. D. Parton, *Dolly*, 59.

23. S. Parton, *Tell It Sister*, 9.

24. Transcript of Warshan Shire's poetry published by Michelle Toglia, https://www.bustle.com/articles/156559-transcript-of-beyonces-lemonade-because-the-words-are-just-as-important-as-the-music. Accessed October 25, 2017.

25. Transcribed from "Loretta Lynn CMA Entertainer of the Year (1974)," https://www.youtube.com/watch?v=0fioCHM-kC0. Accessed October 25, 2017.

26. Loretta Lynn with Patsi Bale Cox, *Still Woman Enough: A Memoir* (New York: Hyperion, 2002), xii.

27. Lynn, *Still Woman Enough*, 10.

28. Lynn, *Still Woman Enough*, 11.

29. Lynn, *Still Woman Enough*, 60.

30. Lynn, *Still Woman Enough*, 62.

31. Lynn, *Still Woman Enough*, 62.

32. Richie, *Compelled to Crime*, 54.

33. Richie, *Compelled to Crime*, 54–55.

34. Michael Arceneaux quoted in Melissa Harris-Perry, "A Call-and-Response with Melissa Harris-Perry: The Pain and the Power of 'Lemonade,'" http://www.elle.com/culture/music/a35903/lemonade-call-and-response/. Accessed October 25, 2017.

35. Louise S. O'Connor, "Henrietta Williams Foster, 'Aunt Rittie': A Cowgirl of the Texas Coastal Bend," in *Black Cowboys of Texas*, ed. Sara R. Massey (College Station: Texas A&M University Press, 200), Kindle Edition loc. 1072–1073.

36. US Works Progress Administration, Federal Writers Project, American LifeHistories: Johanna July. Interview by Florence Angermiller. American Memories Collection, Library of Congress, 1936–1940, http://www.lcweb.loc.gov/. Accessed October 25, 2017.

37. O'Connor, "Henrietta Williams Foster," loc. 1079.

38. Beyoncé, "Daddy Lessons" on *Lemonade* (Parkwood, 2016).

39. *Revelation* 9:21, *biblehub.com*. Accessed October 25, 2017.

40. Christine Nangle on Twitter, https://twitter.com/nanglish/status/724448639293083648. Accessed October 25, 2017.

41. Richie, *Compelled to Crime*, 64–65.

LOVE THE GRIND

1. Beyoncé, "Partition" on *Beyoncé* (Parkwood Entertainment, 2013).

2. Olivia Wilson, "Beyonce's New 'Partition' Video Is So Sexy That

You'll Want to Have Sex with It," http://www.alloy.com/entertain
ment/beyonce-partition-music-video-sexy/. Accessed October 26,
2017.

3. See Kory Grow, "Bill O'Reilly on Beyoncé's 'Partition' Video:
'That's Art?!'" http://www.rollingstone.com/music/news/bill-oreilly
-on-beyonces-partition-video-thats-art-20140311. Accessed October 26, 2017.

4. Cate Young, "* * *Flawless: On 'Beyoncé'; the Album, the Woman,
the Feminist," https://www.cate-young.com/battymamzelle/2013/12
/Flawless-On-Beyonce-The-Album-The-Woman-The-Feminist
.html. Accessed October 26, 2017.

5. Beyoncé, "6 Inch" on *Lemonade* (Parkwood Entertainment, 2016).

6. Beyoncé, "6 Inch."

7. Angelica Jade Bastién, "Breaking Down Beyoncé's Musical Epic
'Lemonade,'" https://www.thrillist.com/entertainment/nation
/beyonce-lemonade-movie-references-connections-and-secrets. Accessed October 26, 2017.

8. Brittney Cooper, Susanna Morris, Robin Boylorn, "Pop Culture:
The Rise of the Ratchet," in *The Crunk Feminist Collection* (New
York: Feminist Press, 2017), Kindle Edition loc. 3980.

9. Cooper et al., "Pop Culture," loc. 3987.

10. See Aisha Durham, "'Check on It': Beyoncé, Southern Booty, and
Black Femininities in Music Video." *Feminist Media Studies* 12:1
(2012), 37–44.

11. Beyoncé, "6 Inch."

12. Martha C. Nussbaum, "'Whether from Reason or Prejudice': Taking
Money for Bodily Services," *Journal of Legal Studies* XXVII (January
1998), 693–694.

13. L. H. Stallings, *Funk the Erotic: Transaesthetics and Black Sexual Cultures* (Urbana, Chicago, and Springfield: University of Illinois Press,
2015), 16.

14. See "Comments" to Amanda Brandeis, "Beyoncé and Rihanna
Inspire UT Feminism Course," http://kxan.com/2014/11/30
/beyonce-and-rihanna-inspire-ut-austin-feminism-course/. Accessed
October 26, 2017.

15. Beyoncé, "Formation" on *Lemonade* (Parkwood Entertainment,
2016).

16. Stallings, *Funk the Erotic*, 16.

17. Karrine Steffans-Short, "'I Am Becky With the Good Hair,'" https://
www.xojane.com/sex/becky-with-good-hair-karrine-steffans-short
-jay-z-hookup. Accessed October 26, 2017.

18. Karrine Steffans, *Confessions of a Video Vixen* (New York: Amistad,
2005), 157–158.

19. Quoted by REIGN time, "Karrine Steffans Is an Alpha Female," https://www.lipstickalley.com/threads/karrine-steffans-is-an-alpha-female.841715/ Accessed October 26, 2017.
20. Cited by Shenequa Golding, "Karrine Steffans on Oprah Winfrey's Childhood: 'She Was a Hoe,'" https://www.vibe.com/2016/03/karrine-steffans-oprah-winfrey-twitter-rant/. Accessed October 26, 2017.
21. Robin Boylorn, "'Brains, Booty, and All Bizness': Identity Politics, Ratchet Respectability, and *The Real Housewives of Atlanta*," in *The Fantasy of Reality: Critical Essays on "The Real Housewives*," ed. Rachel E. Silverman (New York: Peter Lang, 2015), 28, 30.
22. Karrine Steffans, *The Vixen Manual: How to Find, Seduce & Keep the Man You Want* (New York: Grand Central Publishing, 2005), Kindle Edition loc. 2335.
23. Quoted by REIGN time.
24. L. H. Stallings, "Hip Hop and the Black Ratchet Imagination," *Palimpsest: A Journal on Women, Gender, and the Black International* 2:2 (2013), 136.
25. Steffans, "'I Am Becky With the Good Hair.'"
26. Quoted by REIGN time.
27. Kelly E. Hayes, *Holy Harlots: Femininity, Sexuality, and Black Magic in Brazil* (Berkeley: University of California Press, 2011), 60.
28. Hayes, *Holy Harlots*, 201.
29. ConjureMan Ali, "Pomba Gira: Mistress of Witchcraft," http://raven conjure.blogspot.com/2012/07/pomba-gira-mistress-of-witchcraft .html. Accessed October 26, 2017.
30. Ali, "Pomba Gira."
31. Hayes, *Holy Harlots*, 168.
32. Kamaria Roberts and Kenya Downs, "What Beyoncé teaches us about the African Diaspora in 'Lemonade,'" http://www.pbs.org /newshour/art/what-Beyoncé-teaches-us-about-the-african-diaspora -in-lemonade/. Accessed December 6, 2016.
33. Hayes, *Holy Harlots*, 22.
34. Hayes, *Holy Harlots*, 23.
35. Quoted in Kelly Hayes, "Wicked Women and Femmes Fatales: Gender, Power and Pomba Gira in Brazil," *History of Religions* 48:1 (August 2008), 5.
36. Sylvia Obell, "How Blac Chyna Beat the Kardashians at Their Own Game," https://www.buzzfeed.com/sylviaobell/karma -kardashian?utm_term=.dinxRrl5Zn#.xf98KQ6oZ3. Accessed October 26, 2017.
37. "Amber Rose and Black Chyna Make a Statement on the VMA Red Carpet," http://www.mtv.com/video-clips/hu6j15

/vma-2015-amber-rose-and-blac-chyna-make-a-statement-on-the -vma-red-carpet. Accessed October 26, 2017. Transcription mine.

38. Jessica Berson, *The Naked Result: How Exotic Dance Became Big Business* (New York: Oxford University Press, 2016), 65.

39. Quoted in Lola Ogunnaike, "Blac Chyna Bares All," http://www .elle.com/culture/celebrities/a38758/blac-chyna-profile/. Accessed October 26, 2017.

40. Ogunnaike, "Blac Chyna Bares All."

41. Ogunnaike, "Blac Chyna Bares All."

42. Ogunnaike, "Blac Chyna Bares All."

43. *Rob & Chyna* season 1 episode 1, "Are You Still Texting Bitches?" *Bravo*, originally aired September 11, 2016. Transcription mine.

44. Cooper et al., "Pop Culture," loc. 3285.

45. *Rob & Chyna*, "Are You Still Texting Bitches?"

46. Lilith Dorsey, "Pomba Gira and Mary Magdalene: Sacred Whores for the Holidays," https://disqus.com/home/discussion/voodoo universe/pomba_gira_and_mary_magdalene_sacred_whores_for_ the_holiday/oldest/. Accessed October 25, 2017.

47. Quoted in Lily Harrison, "Beyoncé Reveals She Weighed 195 Pounds During Pregnancy, Lost 65 Pounds after Having Blue Ivy," http://www.eonline.com/de/news/494561/beyonce-reveals -she-weighed-195-pounds-during-pregnancy-lost-65-pounds-after -having-blue-ivy. Accessed October 26, 2017.

48. Beyoncé, "6 Inch."

49. Susannah Sharpless, "Beyoncé Killed the Radio Star: A Review of A Visual Album," https://princetonbuffer.princeton.edu/2014/02/14 /beyonce-killed-the-radio-star-a-review-of-a-visual-album/. Accessed October 25, 2017.

50. Sharpless, "Beyoncé."

51. Siren d'Lore, *A Stripper's Handbook: An Ethnographic Portrait of Seven Exotic Dancers* (BookBaby, 2013), 12.

52. Richard Balzer, *Peepshows: A Visual History* (New York: Harry N. Abrams, 1998), 12.

53. Emily J. Lordi, "Beyoncé's Other Women: Considering the Soul Muses of *Lemonade*," http://www.thefader.com/2016/05/06/be yonce-lemonade-women-soul-muses. Accessed October 25, 2017.

54. Robert Farris Thompson, *Flash of the Spirit: African and Afro-American Art and Philosophy* (New York: Vintage, 1984), 74.

55. Beyoncé featuring Nicki Minaj, "* * *Flawless (remix)" (Parkwood Entertainment, 2014).

56. *Love and Hip Hop: Atlanta* season 5, episode 4. Originally aired April 25, 2016, on VH1. Transcription mine.

57. *Love and Hip Hop: Atlanta* season 4, episode 16. Originally aired on

VH1 on August 10, 2015.

58. All citations in this paragraph come from "Joseline's Special Delivery," *Love and Hip Hop: Atlanta*. Originally aired on VH1 on May 1, 2017.

59. Cooper et al., "Pop Culture," loc. 3977.

60. 2Pac Shakur, "Keep Ya Head Up" on *Strictly 4 My N.I.G.G.A.Z.* (Interscope, 1992).

61. Joseline Hernandez quoted by Brittany Lewis, "Joseline Hernandez Reveals Her Troubled Past & Says She'll Never Tweet Another Naked Picture of Herself Again!" https://globalgrind.cassiuslife.com/1862685/joseline-hernandez-reveals-troubled-past-snever-tweet-naked-picture-again-interview/. Accessed October 26, 2017.

62. "Joseline's Special Delivery." Transcription mine.

63. Lordi, "Beyoncé's Other Women."

64. Beyoncé, "6 Inch."

65. Stallings, *Funk the Erotic*, 17.

66. Alecia P. Long, *The Great Southern Babylon: Sex, Race, and Respectability in New Orleans 1865–1920* (Baton Rouge: Louisiana State University Press, 2004), 193.

67. Hayes, "Wicked Women," 5.

68. Audre Lorde, "The Uses of the Erotic: The Erotic as Power," in *Sister Outsider: Essays and Speeches* (Freedom, CA: Freedom Press 2002 [1984]), 55.

UNAPOLOGETICALLY FEMME

1. See the event announcement at http://do512.com/events/2016/8/18/the-beyonce-feminism-sing-along. Accessed March 16, 2017.

2. http://do512.com.

3. Annie Lennox quoted by Laura Stampler, "Annie Lennox: 'Twerking Is Not Feminism,'" http://time.com/3529403/annie-lennox-twerking-feminism/. Accessed December 8, 2016.

4. Janet Mock quoted by Marie Solis, "In Defense of 'Lemonade,' Janet Mock Took a Stand for 'Black Femme Feminists' Everywhere," https://mic.com/articles/143104/in-defense-of-lemonade-janet-mock-took-a-stand-for-black-femme-feminists-everywhere#.Llp6UEeH4. Accessed March 16, 2017.

5. Beyoncé with Nicki Minaj, "* * *Flawless Remix." Lyrics transcribed at https://genius.com/Beyonce-flawless-remix-lyrics. Accessed March 16, 2017.

6. See Gayatri Gopinath, "Queer Regions: Locating Lesbians in Sancharram," in *The Blackwell Companion to Lesbian, Gay, Bisexual,*

Transgender, and Queer Studies, ed. George Haggerty and Molly McGarry (Oxford: Blackwell, 2007), 344.

7. Ashleigh Shakleford, "Hood Femmes and Ratchet Feminism: On Amandla Stenberg, Representation, and #BlackGirlMagic," http://www.forharriet.com/2016/01/hood-femmes-ratchet-feminism-on-amandla.html#axzz4SBiT5tG5. Accessed December 6, 2016.

8. Heather Boener, "Atlanta's Femme Mafia," *Curve* Magazine (March 2007).

9. Boener, "Atlanta's Femme Mafia."

10. Boener, "Atlanta's Femme Mafia."

11. Ulrike Dahl, "White Gloves, Feminist Fists: Race, Nation, and the Feeling of 'Vintage' in Femme Movements," *Gender, Place, and Culture* 21:5 (2014), 604.

12. See https://www.facebook.com/chelsea.johnsonlong. Accessed March 16, 2017.

13. This event description can be found at http://thenichellaverse.tumblr.com/post/135663406042/whereyoufromfrom-yonce-taught-me-femme-of. Accessed March 16, 2017.

14. http://thenichellaverse.tumblr.com.

15. Beyoncé, "Sorry," https://listen.tidal.com/artist/1566/videos#. Accessed December 6, 2016. All references to the video come from this version.

16. On Laolu's "Afromysterics," see Tamara Best, "An Artist Who Uses the Skin as His Canvas," http://www.nytimes.com/2016/11/30/arts/design/a-nigerian-artist-who-uses-the-skin-as-his-canvas.html?_r=1. Accessed December 6, 2016.

17. Sublimefemme, https://sublimefemme.wordpress.com.

18. John Ortved, "Ratchet: The Rap Insult That Became a Compliment," http://nymag.com/thecut/2013/04/ratchet-the-rap-insult-that-became-a-compliment.html. Accessed December 6, 2016.

19. Robert Farris Thompson, "An Aesthetic of the Cool," *African Arts* 7:1 (1973), 41.

20. Chris Kelly, "*Lemonade*: The Hidden Meanings Buried in Beyoncé's Filmic Journey through Grief," http://www.factmag.com/2016/04/27/lemonade-Beyoncé-meaning-visual-album/. Accessed December 6, 2016.

21. Shannon Frystak, *Our Minds on Freedom: Women and the Struggle for Black Equality in Louisiana, 1924–1967* (Baton Rouge: Louisiana State University Press, 2009), 67.

22. Kamaria Roberts and Kenya Downs, "What Beyoncé teaches us about the African Diaspora in 'Lemonade,'" http://www.pbs.org/newshour/art/what-Beyoncé-teaches-us-about-the-african-diaspora-in-lemonade/. Accessed December 6, 2016.

23. See definitions of "chunk the deuce" on Urban Dictionary, http://www.urbandictionary.com/define.php?term=chunk%20a%20deuce. Accessed December 6, 2016.

24. See the comment at http://genius.com/Beyoncé-sorry-lyrics. Accessed December 6, 2016.

25. Brittney Cooper, "Ratchet Feminism," https://crunkfeministcollec tive.wordpress.com/2012/08/14/ratchet-feminism/. Accessed December 6, 2016.

26. See Savannah Shange's bio at http://galleryofthestreets.org/ecohybridity1/. Accessed March 16, 2017.

27. Sonny Oram, "From Reflections: A New Orleans Queer Style Portrait Series," http://www.qwearfashion.com/home/from-reflections -a-new-orleans-queer-style-portrait-series. Accessed March 16, 2017.

28. This portrait can be viewed in Oram, "From Reflections."

29. Savannah Shange, "Black on Purpose: Race, Inheritance, and Queer Reproduction," http://www.thefeministwire.com/2014/10/black-pur pose-race-inheritance-queer-reproduction/. Accessed March 16, 2017.

30. See Savannah's whiteboard reproduced on her website, http://savannahshange.com/teaching/. Accessed March 16, 2017.

31. Beyoncé, "Déjà vu." Viewed at https://listen.tidal.com/video /28504378. Accessed December 7, 2016.

32. Serena Williams quoted by Cindy Boren in "Serena Williams Explains How She Ended Up Twerking in Beyoncé's 'Lemonade,'" https://www.washingtonpost.com/pb/news/early-lead /wp/2016/05/09/serena-williams-explains-how-she-ended-up-twer king-in-Beyoncés-lemonade/?outputType=accessibility&nid=menu_ nav_accessibilityforscreenreader. Accessed December 7, 2016.

33. Anne Mitchell, "Beyoncé as Aggressive Black Femme and Informed Black Female Subject," in *The Beyoncé Effect: Essays on Sexuality, Race, and Feminism*, ed. Adrienne Trier-Bienieck (Jefferson, NC: McFarland & Company, 2016), 42.

34. See Justa Notha's comment on Sasha's post "Aggressive Femme," http://www.cardcarryinglesbian.com/aggressive-femmes. Accessed December 7, 2016.

35. Daniel Peddle, *The Aggressives* (New York: Image Entertainment, 2005).

36. Laine Kaplan-Levenson, "TriPod Mythbusters: Quadroon Balls and Plaçage," http://wwno.org/post/tripod-mythbusters-quadroon-balls -and-pla-age. Accessed December 7, 2016.

37. See Kari Skogland, *The Courage to Love* (New York: Lifetime, 2000), and Peter Medak, *The Feast of All Saints* (New York: Showtime, 2001).

38. Louis Tasistro quoted in Emily Clark, *The Strange History of the American Quadroon: Free Women of Color in the Revolutionary Atlantic World* (Chapel Hill: University of North Carolina Press, 2013), 178.

39. Graham Robb, *Strangers: Homosexual Love in the Nineteenth Century* (New York: W. W. Norton & Company, 2003), 157.

40. Leonard Le'Doux Jr., *The Belles of Chateau Vidal* (CreateSpace Independent Publishing Platform, 2016), 44.

41. Quoted in Noel Voltz, "Black Female Agency and Sexual Exploitation: Quadroon Balls and Plaçage Relationships," senior thesis (Ohio State University, 2008), vii, https://kb.osu.edu/dspace/bitstream /handle/1811/32216/quadroon_balls1.pdf;jsessionid=4BA41EAAF 3D58663303AB3334430E1E4?sequence=1. Accessed December 8, 2016.

42. Mitchell, "Beyoncé."

43. Shamil Tarpischev and Serena Williams quoted in Nolan Feeney, "Serena Williams Blasts Official's 'Sexist' and 'Racist' Remarks," http://time.com/3522553/serena-williams-sexist-racist-shamil -tarpischev/. Accessed December 8, 2016.

44. Serena Williams quoted in Hannah Flint, "Serena Williams: 'I'm Not Sorry for Anything,'" http://lifestyle.one/grazia/celebrity/news /serena-williams-wimbledon-Beyoncé-lemonade/. Accessed December 8, 2016.

45. Serena Williams quoted in Tory Barron, "Serena Williams explains why Beyoncé wanted her in 'Lemonade' video," http://www.espn .com/espnw/culture/the-buzz/article/15499708/serena-williams -explains-why-Beyoncé-wanted-lemonade-video. Accessed December 8, 2016.

46. Danice Brown, "Breaking the Chains: Examining the Endorsement of Modern Jezebel Images and Racial-Ethnic Esteem among African American Women," *Culture, Health, and Society* 15:5 (2013), 526.

47. As of this writing, Austin Graffiti Park is set for demolition and relocation near the airport. See Connor Brown, "Austin Graffiti Park Demolition Approved, Relocation in the Works," https://www .mystatesman.com/news/local/austin-graffiti-park-demolition-ap proved-relocation-the-works/uaTGxx4a62ucPDgm3bAj1M/.

48. Shakia includes a link to a video of the performance on her Facebook page, https://www.facebook.com/ShakiaWilliams27. Accessed March 16, 2017.

49. Graciela Trajtenberg, "Elastic Femininity: How Female Israeli Artists Appropriate a Gender-Endangered Practice," *Frontiers: A Journal of Women's Studies* 37:2 (2016), 167.

50. Gopinath, "Queer Regions," 344.

51. Kyra Gaunt, "YouTube, Twerking & You: Collapse and the Handheld

Co-Presence of Black Girls and Miley Cyrus," *Journal of Popular Music Studies* 27:3 (2015), 247.

52. Gaunt, "YouTube," 253.
53. Quoted by Megan Braden-Perry, "Who Owns Twerking, Who Owns the Bounce? New Orleans Originators Have a Roundtable," http://themuse.jezebel.com/who-owns-twerking-who-owns-the-bounce-new-orleans-ori-1787800363. Accessed March 17, 2017.
54. Braden-Perry, "Who Owns Twerking?"
55. See Gaunt, "YouTube," 256–258.
56. Kimari Carter, personal communication, February 24, 2017.
57. See, for example, the category "Twerking Orgasm" videos on porn hub.com.
58. Janell Hobson, "The 'Batty' Politic: Toward an Aesthetic of the Black Female Body," *Hypatia* 18.4 (Fall/Winter 2003), 102.
59. Thanks to my daughter, Baía Tinsley, for teaching me this rhyme and game.
60. Hobson, "'Batty' Politic," 103.

FREEDOM, TOO

1. Monika Markovinich, "Blue Ivy Accompanies Mom Beyoncé on the 2016 VMAs Red Carpet," http://www.huffingtonpost.ca/entry/beyonce-blue-ivy-mtv-vmas-2016_n_11755076.html. Accessed October 27, 2017.
2. Maeve Keirans, "Beyoncé and Blue Ivy Coordinate on the 2016 VMA Red Carpet," http://www.mtv.com/news/2924910/beyonce-vma-2016-red-carpet/. Accessed October 27, 2017.
3. Victoria M. Massie, "VMA 2016: Beyoncé's VMAs entourage included the Mothers of the Movement," https://www.vox.com/2016/8/29/12685002/mtv-vma-2016-beyonce-black-lives-matter. Accessed October 27, 2017.
4. Beyoncé, "Freedom" on *Lemonade* (Parkwood Entertainment, 2016).
5. Massie, "VMA 2016."
6. Loretta Ross and Rickie Solinger, *Reproductive Justice: An Introduction* (Berkeley: University of California Press, 2017), 72.
7. Beyoncé, "Freedom."
8. Ross and Solinger, *Reproductive Justice*, 69.
9. Beyoncé, "Freedom."
10. Mama Sana/Vibrant Woman, "About," https://www.msvwatx.org/missionvision. Accessed October 27, 2017.
11. MamaSana/Vibrant Woman, "Austin, a 'Family-Friendly' City:

Perspectives and Solutions from Mothers in the City" (2015), iv, https://docs.wixstatic.com/ugd/917d5c_be07366058f4351a27e0d2 391a82752.pdf. Accessed October 27, 2017.

12. MamaSana/Vibrant Woman (2015), 5.

13. MamaSana/Vibrant Woman, https://www.msvwatx.org/history. Accessed October 27, 2017.

14. All quotes from Beyoncé, *Life Is But a Dream* (Parkwood Entertainment, 2013). Transcriptions mine.

15. Beyoncé, "Sorry."

16. Danielle Paquette, "What Beyoncé's 'Lemonade' Means for Women Who Have Miscarried," https://www.washingtonpost.com/news /wonk/wp/2016/04/25/what-beyonces-lemonade-means-for-women -who-have-miscarried/?utm_term=.11b3d7bb5062. Accessed October 27, 2017.

17. Sara R. Cohen on Twitter, https://twitter.com/fertilitylaw/status /724755467545677824. Accessed October 27, 2017.

18. Beyoncé, "Freedom."

19. Laura Seftel, *Grief Unseen: Healing Pregnancy Loss through the Arts* (London and Philadelphia: Jessica Kingsley Publishers, 2006), 18.

20. Beyoncé, "Freedom."

21. Beyoncé, "Freedom."

22. Jenn Hoffman, "Meet the Inspiring Breast Cancer Survivor from Beyoncé's *Lemonade*," http://people.com/celebrity/meet-the-inspir ing-breast-cancer-survivor-from-beyonces-lemonade/. Accessed October 27, 2017.

23. Beyoncé, "Freedom."

24. Lauryn Hill, "Zion" on *The Miseducation of Lauryn Hill* (Columbia Records, 1998).

25. Elizabeth Czukas, "Why Do Black Women Experience More Pregnancy Loss?" https://www.verywell.com/why-do-black-women-have -more-pregnancy-losses-2371724.

26. Hill, "Zion."

27. The Excellence and Advancement Foundation, http://breakthepipe line.com/. Accessed October 27, 2017.

28. "Arrow Child and Family Ministries Annual Report 2016: Creating Outrageous Hope," http://www.arrow.org/downloads/financials /Arrow%202016%20Annual%20Report.pdf. Accessed October 27, 2017.

29. DFPS, "How Big Is the Problem in Child Protective Services?" https://www.dfps.state.tx.us/Child_Protection/Disproportionality /how_big.asp. Accessed October 27, 2017.

30. Beyoncé, "Freedom."

31. Marni Senofonte quoted in Marjon Carlos, "Beyoncé's Stylist Spills

the Juice on the Fashion Behind *Lemonade*," https://www.vogue
.com/article/beyonce-lemonade-stylist-interview-fashion-marni
-senofonte. Accessed October 27, 2017.

32. E. Franklin Frazier, *The Negro Church in America* (New York: Schocken Books, 1974 [1963]), 13.

33. Ross and Solinger, *Reproductive Justice*, 72.

34. Ross and Solinger, *Reproductive Justice*, 193.

35. Beyoncé, "Freedom."

36. Michaela DePrince quoted by Kate Snow, "Against All Odds: Ballerina Michaela DePrince's Remarkable Journey," https://www
.nbcnews.com/news/nbcblk/against-all-odds-ballerina-michaela
-deprince-s-remarkable-journey-n783921. Accessed October 27, 2017.

37. Snow, "Against All Odds."

38. Michaela DePrince with Elaine DePrince, *Taking Flight: From War Orphan to Star Ballerina* (New York: Alfred Knopf, 2014), 167.

39. Tobias Hübinette, "From Orphan Trains to Babylifts: Colonial Trafficking, Empire Building, and Social Engineering," in *Outsiders Within: Writing on Transracial Adoption*, ed. Jane Jeong Trenka, Julia Chinyere Oparah, and Sun Yung Shin (Cambridge, MA: South End Press, 2006), 142–143.

40. Lezley McSpadden, "Michael Brown's Mom on Sterling Brown and Philando Castile," https://www.nytimes.com/2016/07/08/opinion /michael-browns-mom-on-alton-sterling-and-philando-castile.html. Accessed October 27, 2017.

41. Lezley McSpadden quoted by Naja Rayne, "Mother of Michael Brown Talks about Her Cameo in Beyoncé's 'Lemonade,'" http:// people.com/celebrity/mother-of-michael-brown-talks-about-her -cameo-in-beyonces-lemonade/. Accessed October 27, 2017.

42. Marla Frederick, *Between Sundays: Black Women and Everyday Struggles of Faith* (Berkeley: University of California Press, 2003), 28.

43. Michaela DePrince quoted by Desiree Murphy, "Ballerina Michaela DePrince on Her Personal Journey to 'Freedom' in Beyonce's 'Lemonade,'" http://www.etonline.com/features/188266_beyonce_lemon ade_ballerina_michaela_deprince_set_secrets_personal_freedom_ journey. Accessed October 27, 2017.

44. Murphy, "Ballerina Michaela DePrince."

45. Beyoncé, "Freedom."

46. Ross and Solinger, *Reproductive Justice*, 72.

47. Dorothy Roberts, *Shattered Bonds: The Color of Child Welfare* (New York: Civitas, 2002), 8.

48. Roberts, 35.

49. Stephanie Clifford and Jessica Silver-Greenberg, "Foster Care as

Punishment: The New Reality of 'Jane Crow,'" https://www.nytimes.com/2017/07/21/nyregion/foster-care-nyc-jane-crow.html. Accessed October 27, 2017.

50. Alex Haley, *The Autobiography of Malcolm X* (New York: Ballentine Books, 2002 [1964]), 25.

51. http://allgo.org/. Accessed October 27, 2017.

52. http://allgo.org/blog/. Accessed October 27, 2017.

53. Beyoncé, "Freedom."

54. Ross and Solinger, *Reproductive Justice*, 72.

55. Quoted by Alexander Abad-Santos, "No One Liked The Onion's Quevenzhane Wallis 'Joke,'" https://www.theatlantic.com/entertainment/archive/2013/02/onion-quevenzhane-wallis-joke/318001/. Accessed October 27, 2017.

56. Mia McKenzie, *Black Girl Dangerous on Race, Queerness, Class and Gender* (BGD Press), Kindle loc. 1447–1448.

57. Sika Dagbovie-Evans, "Pigtails, Ponytails, and Getting Tail: The Infantilization and Hypersexualization of African American Females in Popular Culture," *Journal of Popular Culture* 46:4 (2013), 746.

58. McKenzie, *Black Girl Dangerous*, loc. 1448–1449.

59. Amandla Stenberg quoted by Isis Briones, "Beyoncé Compliments Amandla Stenberg in the Best Way," https://www.teenvogue.com/story/beyonce-blue-ivy-compliment-to-amandla-stenberg. Accessed October 27, 2017.

60. Amandla Stenberg, "Don't Cashcrop My Cornrows," https://www.youtube.com/watch?v=O1KJRRSB_XA. Accessed October 27, 2017.

61. Amandla Stenberg quoted by Abby Aguirre, "Amandla Stenberg is a Voice for the Future," https://www.vogue.com/article/amandla-stenberg-interview-gender-feminism-black-culture. Accessed October 27, 2017.

62. McKenzie, *Black Girl Dangerous*, loc. 1439–1441.

63. Beyoncé, "Freedom."

I CAME TO SLAY

1. Big Freedia in *Big Freedia: Queen of Bounce* season 4, episode 3, "Omg it's Beyonce!" Originally aired June 23, 2016, on Fuse. Transcription mine.

2. Big Freedia quoted by Gina Vivinetto, "Big Freedia: This Queen Will Make You Bounce," https://www.advocate.com/arts-entertainment/music/2015/04/01/big-freedia-queen-will-make-you-bounce. Accessed October 28, 2017.

3. Big Freedia in *Big Freedia: Queen of Bounce* season 4, episode 1, "Freedia Takes Manhattan." Originally aired October 1, 2015, on Fuse. Transcription mine.

4. Big Freedia in "Omg it's Beyonce!" Transcription mine.

5. Beyoncé, "Formation" on *Lemonade* (Parkwood Entertainment, 2016).

6. Zandria Robinson, "We Slay, Part I," https://newsouthnegress.com /southernslayings/. Accessed October 28, 2017.

7. Big Freedia in "Freedia Takes Manhattan." Transcription mine.

8. Treva Ellison, Kai Greene, Matt Richardson, and C. Riley Snorton, "We Got Issues: Toward a Black Trans*/Studies," *TSQ: Transgender Studies Quarterly* 4.2 (May 2017), 164.

9. RuPaul's Drag Race Dictionary, http://rupaulsdragrace.wikia.com /wiki/RuPaul%27s_Drag_Race_Dictionary#S/. Accessed October 28, 2017.

10. Marlon Bailey, *Butch Queens up in Pumps: Gender, Performance, and Ballroom Culture in Detroit* (Ann Arbor: University of Michigan Press, 2013), 116.

11. Big Freedia in "Omg it's Beyonce!" Transcription mine.

12. Beyoncé, "Love Drought" on *Lemonade* (Parkwood Entertainment, 2016).

13. Garnet Coleman quoted by W. Gardner Selby, "Garnet Coleman Said Transgender Individuals Have a 1 in 12 Chance of Getting Murdered," http://www.politifact.com/texas/statements/2015 /may/13/garnet-coleman/garnet-coleman-said-transgender-person -has-1-12-ch/. Accessed October 28, 2017. Coleman has since conceded that this statistic is unverifiable, while holding to his larger point that trans* folk are attacked at rates that far exceed those of their cis counterparts.

14. Beyoncé, "Love Drought."

15. Laverne Cox in "Laverne Cox: Beyoncé Helped Me Come into My Womanhood," https://www.essence.com/video/laverne-cox -beyonce-grammys-womanhood. Accessed October 28, 2018.

16. Laverne Cox quoted by Nicole Sands, "Laverne Cox on Grammy Metallica Mishap: 'It Was on the Teleprompter and I Was in a Moment," http://people.com/music/grammys-2017-laverne-cox -metallica-mishap-explaination/. Accessed October 28, 2017.

17. Laverne Cox with David Hochman, "Laverne Cox Is One Luminous Lady," http://www.cbs.com/shows/watch_magazine /archive/1006796/laverne-cox-is-one-luminous-lady/. Accessed October 28, 2017.

18. Laverne Cox quoted by Katy Steinmetz, "Laverne Cox Talks to TIME about the Transgender Movement," http://time.com/132769

/transgender-orange-is-the-new-black-laverne-cox-interview/. Accessed October 28, 2017.

19. Steinmetz, "Laverne Cox."

20. Laverne Cox quoted by Melanie Smith, "#MotivationMonday: 15 Times Laverne Cox Dropped Inspiration on Us All," https://global grind.cassiuslife.com/4075912/laverne-cox-inspirational-quotes/. Accessed October 28, 2017.

21. Laverne Cox quoted by Diane Gordon, "Laverne Cox: 'Trans Rights Are Women's Rights,'" https://www.thecut.com/2017/02 /laverne-cox-trans-rights-are-womens-rights.html. Accessed October 28, 2017.

22. Laverne Cox quoted by Zack Ford, "Laverne Cox: 'Loving Trans People Is a Revolutionary Act,'" https://thinkprogress.org/laverne -cox-loving-trans-people-is-a-revolutionary-act-2b79c142ae69/. Accessed October 28, 2017.

23. Laverne Cox at Creating Change 2014. Transcript at http:// letsbowbtches.tumblr.com/post/75579314133/laverne-cox-at -creating-change-2014-transcript. Accessed October 28, 2017.

24. Laverne Cox quoted by Ted Kerr, "AIN'T I A WOMAN—Asks Laverne Cox, Actress, Producer and Transgender advocate," https:// www.visualaids.org/blog/detail/aint-i-a-woman-asks-laverne-cox -actress-producer-and-transgender-advocate. Accessed October 28, 2017.

25. Beyoncé quoted by Maddy Budd, "Beyonce Surprised Laverne Cox with the Sweetest Gift," http://www.harpersbazaar.com/celebrity /latest/news/a18543/laverne-cox-received-a-beautiful-gift-from -beyonce/. Accessed October 28, 2017.

26. Beyoncé, "Formation."

27. Beyoncé, "Formation."

28. Jennifer Declue, "To Visualize the Queen Diva! Toward Black Feminist Transinclusivity in Beyoncé's 'Formation,'" *TSQ/Transgender Studies* 4.2 (May 2017), 220.

29. Willi Coleman, "Among the Things That Used to Be" in Barbara Smith, ed., *Home Girls: A Black Feminist Anthology* (New York: Kitchen Table, Women of Color Press, 1983), 221–222.

30. Alix Chapman, "The Punk Show: Queering Heritage in the Black Diaspora," *Cultural Studies* 26:3 (2014), 339.

31. Alix Chapman, "The Body Rockers: New Orleans 'Sissy' Bounce and the Politics of Displacement," PhD diss. (University of Texas at Austin, 2013), 105.

32. Chapman, "Body Rockers," 107.

33. Ginetta Candelario, "Hair Race-ing: Dominican Beauty Culture and Identity Production," *Meridians* 1 (2000), 152.

34. Beyoncé, "Hold Up" on *Lemonade* (Parkwood Entertainment, 2016).
35. Quoted by Omise'eke Tinsley, "Let's Celebrate Black Trans Women's Lives, Not Deaths," https://www.advocate.com/commentary/2015/10/27/lets-celebrate-black-trans-womens-lives-not-deaths. Accessed October 28, 2017.
36. CeCe McDonald, "Afro Innovation: Re-Imagining Black Genders" (presented at Mapping the Afro Imaginative: Black Queer Studies and the Work of the Imagination, University of Texas at Austin, March 5, 2015).
37. Beyoncé, "Hold Up."
38. Janet Mock, *Redefining Realness: My Path to Womanhood, Identity, Love & So Much More* (New York: Atria, 2014), 75.
39. Mock, *Redefining Realness*, 76.
40. Mock, *Redefining Realness*, 76.
41. Mock, *Redefining Realness*, 65.
42. Mock, *Redefining Realness*, 65.
43. Mock, *Redefining Realness*, 65.
44. Mock, *Redefining Realness*, 66.
45. Mock, *Redefining Realness*, 193.
46. Janet Mock quoted by Hilton Dresden, "Trans Advocate Janet Mock on *Lemonade*, New Memoir, and Advice to Twentysomethings," https://www.out.com/popnography/2016/7/27/trans-advocate-janet-mock-lemonade-new-memoir-advice-twentysomethings. Accessed October 29, 2019.
47. Bell Hooks, "Moving Beyond Pain," http://www.bellhooksinstitute.com/blog/2016/5/9/moving-beyond-pain. Accessed October 29, 2017.
48. Janet Mock, https://www.facebook.com/janetmock/posts/10154228113096522. Accessed October 29, 2017.
49. Beyoncé, "Formation."
50. Cecil W. Carter quoted by Edward F. Haas, *Mayor Victor H. Schiro: New Orleans in Transition, 1961–1970* (Jackson: University Press of Mississippi, 2014), 282.
51. Beyoncé, "Formation."
52. Beyoncé, "Formation."
53. This can be accessed at https://www.facebook.com/janetmock/photos/a.10151901670486522.1073741825.375092221521/10152360681966522/?type=1.
54. Julia Serano, *Excluded: Making Feminist and Queer Movements More Inclusive* (New York: Seal Press, 2013), 62.
55. Adisa Gooding, https://www.facebook.com/adisag. Accessed October 29, 2017.

56. Adisa Gooding, quoted in "Serving Truth," *Dance Mogul* (July 17, 2016), http://dancemogul.com/news/?p=8691. Accessed October 29, 2017.

57. Miss Shalae quoted by Lucy Tiven, "These Transgender Artists Found a Way to Make 'Lemonade' Even More Empowering," https://www.attn.com/stories/10056/transgender-remake-of -beyonce-lemonade. Accessed October 29, 2017.

58. Tiven, "These Transgender Artists."

59. Miss Shalae and Adisa Gooding, "Lemonade Served Bitter-sweet," https://www.facebook.com/miss.shalae.michaels/videos /204341396629398/. Accessed October 29, 2017.

60. Dora Silva Santana, "Transitionings and Returnings: Experiments with the Poetics of Transatlantic Water," *TSQ* 4:2 (May 2017), 183.

61. Yuriel Young/Miss Shalae, "Untitled," https://www.facebook.com /yuriel.young/posts/614118888781701. Accessed October 29, 2017.

62. Miss Shalae on Instagram, https://www.instagram.com/p/BQBd 9fOlLPf/?taken-by=miss_shalae. Accessed October 29, 2017.

63. Azizi Powell, "What '___ Gives Me Life' Means (Slang Meanings)," http://pancocojams.blogspot.com/2015/03/what-someone-or-some thing-gives-me-life.html. Accessed October 29, 2017.

64. Miss Shalae quoted by Miranda Bryant, "'She Is an Inspiration': Transgender Women Recreate Beyoncé's Lemonade Video in a Bid for Other Trans People to 'Follow Their Hearts and Dreams,'" http://www.dailymail.co.uk/femail/article-3692724/She-inspiration -Transgender-women-recreate-Beyonce-s-stunning-Lemonade -video-bid-inspire-trans-people-follow-hearts-dreams.html#ixzz 4pI4R7Iol. Accessed October 29, 2017.

65. Julie Compton, "Deadly Hurricane Exposes Dangers of Being LGBTQ and Homeless," https://www.nbcnews.com/feature /nbc-out/hurricane-harvey-exposes-dangers-being-lgbtq-home less-n799126. Accessed October 29, 2017.

66. Compton, "Deadly Hurricane."

OUTRO

1. "Happy Birthday Beyoncé," https://www.beyonce.com/bday2017/. Accessed February 11, 2018.

2. Jay Z and Gloria Carter, "Smile" on *4:44* (ROC Nation, 2017).

3. Gloria Carter on "D'USSÉ Friday: The Gloria Carter Episode," https://listen.tidal.com/artist/9366612/videos. Accessed February 11, 2018. Transcription mine.

4. Jay Z and Gloria Carter, "Smile."

5. G. Carter, "D'USSÉ Friday."
6. Alaina Monts, "Gloria Carter, Blue Ivy's Grandma, Comes Out as a Lesbian on Jay Z's '4:44,'" https://www.autostraddle.com/gloria -carter-blue-ivys-grandma-comes-out-as-a-lesbian-on-jay-zs-444 –384764/. Accessed February 11, 2018.
7. Sarah Kate Ellis quoted by Sabrina Finkelstein, "GLAAD Hails Jay-Z's Mom for Coming Out as a Lesbian," https://www.billboard.com /articles/news/7850122/jay-z-mom-lesbian-gloria-carter-smile-glaad. Accessed February 11, 2018.
8. Tiq Milan quoted by Da'Shan Smith, "The Importance of Jay Z's 'Smile' & Its Progression of LGBTQ Politics in Hip Hop," https:// www.billboard.com/articles/news/pride/7881034/jay-z-444-smile -mom-transgender-lgbtq-politics-hip-hop. Accessed February 11, 2018.
9. Sandra Rose, "Shawn 'Jay Z' Carter's 'Other' Mom Works for His Foundation," http://sandrarose.com/2013/11/shawn-jay-z-carters -other-mom-works-for-his-foundation/. Accessed February 11, 2018.
10. Rose, "Shawn 'Jay Z.'"
11. Eurpublisher, "Kimberly Gossip! Jay Z's 2 Moms and Missing Moola," http://archive.eurweb.com/2013/11/kimberly-gossip-jay-zs -2-moms-and-missing-moola-kevin-terry-new-atls-vawn/#. Accessed February 11, 2018.
12. Hollywood Street King, "Gloria Carter's Lesbian Life Partner Uncovered," https://hollywoodstreetking.com/jay-zs-got-two-parents -and-a-father-aint-one-gloria-carters-lesbian-life-partner-uncovered/. Accessed February 11, 2018.
13. Candice Lyons, personal communication, February 7, 2018.
14. William Mosley, personal communication, February 9, 2018.
15. William Mosley, personal communication, February 8, 2018.
16. Jacqueline Smith, personal communication, February 7, 2018.
17. Jarvis Dillard, personal communication, February 9, 2018.
18. Kara Keeling, *The Witch's Flight: The Cinematic, the Black Femme, and the Image of Common Sense* (Durham, NC: Duke University Press, 2007), 142.
19. Keeling, *Witch's Flight*, 143.
20. Beyoncé, "Suga Mama" on *B-day* (Columbia Records, 2006).

INDEX

8091